Have a Great Midlife Crisis

By

John Bryan Stone

It's time to become

the man you've always wanted to be.

Have a Great Midlife Crisis

Copyright © 2008 by John Bryan Stone

All rights reserved. No part of this publication may be reproduced or transmitted in any form or by any means, electronic or mechanical, including photocopy, recording or any information and retrieval system, without permission in writing from the copyright holder/publisher, except in the case of brief quotations embodied in critical articles reviews.

ISBN 978-1-4357-4254-3

Author's website: www.ManUpMen.wordpress.com

Acknowledgements

It's not easy becoming your own man in today's disposable society, where men who are just reaching their full power are often thrown away, overlooked and even ridiculed. This book would not be possible without the wise insights, long discussions, and painful living experiences shared with my great friend, T. B. I have used your initials to protect your privacy, but you know who you are. You saved my life. I like to think the purpose of that was to help me save other men's lives. Thank you.

John Bryan Stone

Disclaimer

Use of this book and related websites and all affiliated sites is entirely at the risk and discretion of the user.

The author cannot warrant ANY of the information in this book or on related or affiliated sites, and can make no guarantees as to its accuracy or as to the rationality of any of the opinions expressed.

Every effort has been made to ensure that no physical harm or mental anguish results from the use of this book or its related or affiliated websites. Nevertheless, users are advised to use this book and related or affiliated websites responsibly and users are reminded again and again that the author accepts no responsibility for any damage and harm caused by use of the information in this book or in related or affiliated websites.

User acknowledges that user will take responsibility for his or her actions and will under no circumstances hold the author responsible for any damage resulting to user or anyone else from use of this book or its related or affiliated websites.

THE PURCHASER AND/OR USER OF THE BOOK, NEWSLETTERS, WEBSITES, AND ANY RELATED MATERIALS ASSUMES TOTAL RESPONSIBILITY AND RISK FOR USE OF THE BOOK, NEWSLETTERS, WEB-SITES, AND ANY OTHER SITE ACCESSIBLE THROUGH THESE SITES, AND ANY RELATED PRODUCTS OR SERVICES.

INFORMATION CONTAINED IN THE BOOK, NEWSLETTERS, WEBSITES AND RELATED MATERIALS ARE INTENDED AS AN EDUCATIONAL AID ONLY. INFORMATION IS NOT INTENDED AS MEDICAL ADVICE FOR INDIVIDUAL CONDITIONS OR TREATMENT AND IS NOT A SUBSTITUTE FOR A MEDICAL EXAMINATION, NOR DOES IT REPLACE THE NEED FOR SERVICES PROVIDED BY MEDICAL PROFESSIONALS OR INDEPENDENT DETERMINATIONS.

INFORMATION IS NOT INTENDED AS FINANCIAL OR LEGAL ADVICE FOR INDIVIDUAL CIRCUMSTANCES AND IS NOT A SUBSTITUTE FOR PROFESSIONAL FINANCIAL OR LEGAL ADVICE NOR DOES IT REPLACE THE NEED FOR SERVICES PROVIDED BY FINANCIAL ADVISORS, ATTORNEYS, OR INDEPENDENT DETERMINATIONS.

THE PUBLISHER OR ITS OWNERS, SPONSORS, SITE DEVELOPERS, OR AGENTS DO NOT ASSUME ANY RESPONSIBILITY OR RISK FOR THE USE OF ANY INFORMATION CONTAINED WITHIN THE BOOK.

Copyright

Copyright in all material (including text and images) is owned by John Bryan Stone or his licensors and all rights in respect of the same are reserved. No material in this book on affiliated or related sites may be modified, reproduced or transmitted in any medium without the author's express prior written permission, save for personal, non-commercial use through the internet and transient production on screen by such persons for such purposes.

Copyright © 2008 by John Bryan Stone

Contents

Introduction	This is the Only Midlife Crisis You Get	7
Chapter One	Extra Women	11
Chapter Two	Extra Money	23
Chapter Three	Extra Creativity	41
Chapter Four	Extra Fun—Toys and Adventures	48
Chapter Five	Extra Health—Become Your Best	57
Chapter Six	Extra Commitments for Your Marriage	70
Chapter Seven	Extramarital—Divorce Protection	78
Chapter Eight	Extra Caution—Spy Stuff	89
Chapter Nine	Extra Inspiration—How You'll Look Back	102
Chapter Ten	Your Midlife Master Plan	107
Appendix	Extra Resources to Make Midlife Better	124

Introduction

This is the Only Midlife Crisis You Get.

Let's make it count!

Nobody takes you seriously. They say you're going through a phase, and it will pass. Some even say you're being childish, selfish.

They say you're having a midlife crisis, but they say "crisis" with a wink. Nobody considers it a real crisis.

Nobody but you.

You know your pain is real. You know your despair is overwhelming. You're not some pitiful middle-aged man trying to relive his adolescence. You're mourning the death of your dreams.

You and I are not going to let those dreams die. We're going to do something about it.

You're having a midlife crisis for a reason. It's not a silly phase to be made fun of; it's a wakeup call to be listened to.

The people around you won't listen, so you'll have to. Listen to yourself. What was it you were going to be? What was it you were going to do? Where is the man you dreamed of becoming?

He's still in there, screaming to get out, waking you in the middle of the night, tugging at your heart, saying, "Don't let me die!"

You and I, we're not going to let him die. We're going to empower that great man inside you. We're going to face down the critics and naysayers, the ones who don't want you to change.

Of course they don't want you to change. They're counting on you to stay the same. They make your dependability sound noble. Good ol' you. They can always count on you to buck up and slog through your misery without complaining. They can depend on you to stick with it no matter how boring and numbing your life is. Good ol' you. Good ol' you is dying inside.

I know, you're *this* close to telling everyone to go to hell, quitting your job and disappearing to Tahiti with that girl you've had your eye on. But let's face it, at this point in your life you can't afford to screw up. This is it. You've got to make your move and it's got to work.

So let's make a plan. Let's think this thing through and come up with some ideas for getting the life back into your life for the rest of your life.

No, it's not too late. That voice saying it's too late doesn't come from the strong you. That's the weak little victim who has allowed other people's demands to drain him. They want the victim in you to believe it's too late, because they're not through taking what they want from you.

Sure, you've got obligations, and you're a good man, not the type to just run out on your responsibilities. So quit shirking your responsibility—to yourself!

And you have another responsibility besides to yourself. You owe the world a better you. It's not just you that you're cheating. Somebody out there needs the you that you've hidden away. Whether it's love, talent, brains or spirit, believe me, the world needs more of what you've got.

In the following pages we'll think through everything—the exciting stuff, the embarrassing stuff, the scary stuff. All the thoughts and feelings you thought no one else was having. And we're not just going to indulge your whims; we'll challenge you to pursue your deepest longings.

What if this was the beginning of the greatest year of your life? What if you had the most success, the best sex, the most optimistic outlook and the greatest plan for your life?

You only get one midlife crisis. Why not have a *great* midlife crisis?

Go to www.ManUpMen.wordpress.com to learn more about how you can come alive as a man and win!

My friendly reminder:

I'm not having a crisis, I'm having an adventure!

Chapter One

Extra Women.

Get more women in your life!

You can measure a man's wealth by the number of women in his life. You see them all the time—rich guys surrounded by women. Not necessarily women they're sleeping with, but lots of female companions, friends and admirers.

"Sure," you say, "they attract women because they're rich."

But what if it's the opposite? What if they're rich because they attract women? Men do better in life when women find them attractive.

Want to know why?

Because women are usually the shoppers. They drive most of the buying in our economy.

When women see other women hanging on the arms of a man, they think, "This guy has something to offer. I should pay attention to him."

Men think, "I want to be like that guy. He sure has it together."

When people feel this way about you, they want to do business with you. And when people do business with you, you are prosperous.

11

You may say, "It's not just attracting women; it's attracting *people*." Yeah, but guys who tend to hang around with guys are followers. They run in packs, following the Alpha Male. And guess what? That Alpha Male attracts women. That's why all those guys hang around him!

He attracts women, money, and prosperity.

So get out of the pack and step out front where the ladies can see you.

Now you may be worried about your looks. Before you start dressing like a teen and sporting a bad comb-over, stop and realize you already have what women want. Lucky for you, it's not your looks that will get you women. It's power. Power includes money, experience, wisdom and passion. Women will flock to you if you have any of these. If you've survived to middle age, you've got what women are attracted to: the power to survive, make it, and take charge.

So take charge. But be warned, Mr. Powerful. There's one thing I can almost guarantee: at least one woman in your life thinks she has the right to dictate whether you can have extra women around you. Be certain she'll try to embarrass you back into line if she catches you. Only you can decide whether her "hurt" over your actions is enough to stop you from doing what you want to do. One of the ways people try to control you is by feeling hurt by your actions. And not just actions involving other women; but anything you do to expand and improve your life. It goes something like this: "It hurt me that you went out with the guys after work." Or, "It really hurt when I saw you looking at that other woman," or, "I can't believe you would hurt your family by even *thinking* of changing jobs." Translation: It hurts me when you don't let me control you.

How come you never say things like, "It hurts me when you object to me going out with the guys," or, "It hurts me when you get angry just because I notice another woman?" How about, "It hurts me that you would want me to stick with a job that is killing my soul."

Don't bother saying all these things. Our society likes to keep men down so they won't get too rowdy. They want order so much, they will sacrifice your needs.

And if those needs have anything to do with having more women around you, you're in for a big put-down. You know the cliché--you're just another horny guy looking for excuses to get out of control. Baloney. If you've been thinking about more women, it's not because you can't control yourself. It's because you're being controlled. You need something and someone doesn't want you to have it. I know you don't want to hurt anyone, but you don't want to die of starvation either. This is real. This is your life.

Many people don't mind watching you cut yourself to shreds on your broken dreams, as long as they don't lose control of you. It's as if they're saying, "Dance on glass if you want, but just keep dancing to my tune."

Well you don't have to dance to their tune. You can start asking for what you want.

So what do you want? If you want more women in your life, don't be embarrassed. Wanting lots of women is built into your genes. It's the reason humanity has survived. Your desire for extra women is an ancient urge.

Women have an equally ancient urge to keep just one man around for protection.

What is *not* ancient is women telling men their urges are not acceptable. It's hard to say how this arrangement got started, but you don't have to participate in this craziness.

If I were writing this for your mate, I would say, "It's natural to feel attracted to other women, as long as you don't act on it." Hey, if you want to, show her that sentence. She'll approve and maybe even give you permission to read the rest of this book. Those of you who don't need permission, read on.

Some women boil it down to "Look, but don't touch." Well thank you very much! I'm glad you have decided which of *my* senses I can use.

Here's an idea. Get out there and bring *all* your senses back to life. Look at what you want to look at, savor the perfume, taste delicacies, listen to sweet voices calling your name, and touch beauty.

It'll be our secret. Actually, three secrets.

The Three Secrets about Extra Women

Secret Number One: You don't have to stop loving your wife to want other women.

The rules of our society say you have to get a divorce to even go find out if you want more attention, sex, or affection. Wow. You are supposed to risk everything just to find out! What if you go out there and find out you want what you had? There's no healthy reason to play such a high stakes game.

Imagine saying, "Honey, I want a divorce. I really want to see the Starbucks barista naked, so here's half my income and assets."

And what about just having female friends? Even *that* is restricted! Know why? Because if you become more powerful, you could break the hold of the person controlling you. And one of the ways to become more powerful is to have more women around you. If that

14

person finds out you are expanding your female contacts, the next thing you know, you'll be deciding what you want to do with your life, and we can't have that!

So let's just make it our little secret. Some men find it perfectly acceptable to love their mates and have extra women on the side. Still others do some experimenting, only to discover it was not what they expected, and they go back to their previous arrangement. Don't destroy your life just to find out.

Maybe you made a vow to "forsake all others." Maybe it was a foolish vow. You don't have to be bound by the decisions of a wide-eyed, love-struck groom. Let's make sure you don't forsake yourself.

You don't have to stop loving anybody just because you have some fresh desires. If she doesn't love you enough to let you do what you need to, just keep it to yourself. Be bigger about it. Love her even if she is still wrapped up in adolescent fantasies of "possessing" someone for life.

Secret Number Two: Sex without love is fulfilling.

One of the most common cultural myths is that lovemaking is more satisfying than "meaningless" sex. What a scam. Come on, lovemaking can be tedious, too slow, and disappointing. Why do you always have to be in the mood for glow-and-cuddle lovemaking?

Maybe that's what is wrong at home. No sex, all lovemaking. Where's the animal attraction? Where's the not-so-nice bump and grind?

You can try to stay faithful by asking your wife to try new things in bed. She's probably read an article in a women's magazine about this. Most of these ideas will seem pretty lame, but maybe if you try her way she will try yours. From toys to dirty talk, you can try some things out. At some point, she may ask if you only want sex or do you want to make love. Ah oh, end of experimentation. Negotiations over. Sigh, make love, and forget about that exciting new sex life. She didn't even stick with a new position without hinting that sex is bad, love is good.

Oh, well, let's admit one thing. Half the fun of lust is that you're lusting after someone new. It's the newness that accounts for the appeal. You're going to have to decide what you're willing to live without, and whether you're going to die wondering about that Starbucks barista. And her twin sister.

Don't let anyone tell you there is something wrong with lust. It's one of the great things about being alive. Don't you ever let anyone shame you out of such a wonderful feeling!

And dammit, sex without love is perfectly fulfilling. It doesn't have to feel "empty." It's not "meaningless." Oh and how about "soulless?" The only thing soulless is asking you to live the rest of your life clenching your teeth over unfulfilled desires.

Secret Number Three: There are people who are willing to destroy you to keep you from living your life fully.

Don't start blurting out what you really want in life. Modern males are expected to "take it like a man" and just do without. It's been a woman's world for decades now. You are expected to provide, change, go to counseling and do anything it takes to make your woman happy.

Be careful. I'm not saying people will simply disapprove of your natural desires to live more of your life. I'm saying they will destroy you for those desires. They will smile while they watch you lose your house, your job, your status and your future.

Lots of people take sadistic pleasure in watching a man get "caught" acting out his desires. They'll pass the word, put your name online, and tell everyone they can that you lack "character."

"Character" is defined by them, of course. It means sacrificing yourself; not doing what you really want. Just once wouldn't you like to hear, "He showed such character by going for what he wanted in life, and not letting anyone stand in his way"?

Now I can't tell you what to do about your desires for extra women. If you want to set those desires aside, I can respect that, as long as it's your decision, and not something that is dictated by someone else.

And if you decide to explore, I urge you protect your lifestyle, reputation and income. This is a tough task because it's so damn sneaky. And you're probably not the sneaky type. I get it. But PLEASE don't risk everything just to find out if what you are feeling is genuine. If you really feel compelled to tell all in advance, I highly recommend you just skip these desires for now. If you decide to explore, you're going to have to get comfortable with keeping things to yourself.

"But that's lying and cheating!" I can hear the objections now. Stick with me here, I want to show you something.

Look at how our society picks and chooses when it's okay to lie.

Here's an example: One of the top recommendations for job interviews is to never put down your old boss. You won't get hired if you complain about your former employer. Headhunters recommend you say the reason you left is something like, "I was looking for new growth opportunities."

In other words, lie. Don't tell the real truth. Why? Because your survival is at stake. You need the new job, and blurting out the truth that your old boss was an ass will violate job-hunting etiquette. You'll be ruined financially if you tell the truth.

So why are you supposed to blurt out your true desires for women? Try it, and you'll be ruined, just like telling the truth in the interview will bring your career to a dead stop.

Quit whining that nobody understands you. People who need to be understood always struggle at the bottom, begging for their superiors to listen to them. Understand yourself. Tell yourself the truth. Email me if you want to. Just don't feel guilty for protecting yourself by keeping some things secret. Man up. Get what you need.

Now we're going to do this with some class. You'll be able to write to me and honestly say that you acted like a Man-Up Man if you avoid the three U's: Underage, Unwilling, and Undercover.

Underage. Your activities will be limited to consenting adults. Don't try to convince me you're a man if you hurt children. Anyone under legal age is a child. Man-Up Men protect children.

Unwilling. I said *consenting* adults. Force is not manly. It is brutality—as in brutes do it, not men.

Undercover. You can buy a woman dinner, hoping to have sex. You can fix her car, do her taxes, or hook up her cable TV. The Sex Police approve of bartering. But if you pay cash, you're under arrest. Guys whose sex life is paid for in cash always get busted eventually.

Okay, those are the ground rules. I know, you may not be used to planning out your sex life, but trust me, it beats putting yourself in a position where someone has the power to ruin you.

The people who think they have a right to control you will catch up to you if:

1. **You use your real name.** You just gave away your right to privacy.
2. **You pay for sex.** Now the government is interested, and you've increased the number of snoopers tenfold.
3. **You use credit cards.** Everything is on record—where you were, when you paid, how much and how often.

4. **You use your home or office for meetings.** Other people control these locations, and they will come after you if you violate their space with sexual activity.
5. **You put details in emails or snail mail.** Now there's a record of your activities in someone else's hands.
6. **You make decisions while drunk.** "Going for it" when your judgment is impaired is a surefire way to lose.
7. **You use household money.** If someone thinks your earnings are hers to budget, then trips, dinners, even ice cream cones with a new friend will catch your mate's attention.
8. **You brag to friends.** Now you've spread the word, and the more people who know, the more people who can slip up and devastate you.
9. **You make your labor into love.** Stay away from coworkers. Too much gossip, too much risk.
10. **You fail to plan.** Think through your activities. Assess the risk in advance. Weigh it against the rewards. Cover your butt.

So now you can rate your risk on a scale of 1 to 10.

For example, if someone knows your real name (#1), you've been emailing that someone (#5), and your friend knows about it (#8), you've got a risk factor of 3.

If you meet a coworker (#9) for drinks (#6), then alcohol and camaraderie take things further than you anticipated, and you send flowers with a note (#5) paid for with a credit card (#3), you have a risk factor of 4. You might rate it a 5 since she knows your real name.

So what's acceptable risk? Start with zero. Especially if you're new at this. It's not that hard to plan ahead and eliminate most or all of the threats.

If you're already in a situation, rate the risk now and decide if the risk is worth it. Don't evaluate the situation when you're all worked up either. You'll imagine the reward is worth any risk. Say you rate it a 7. Look out. You are in jeopardy. Withdraw from the battle field and live to fight another day.

Let me give you a good starting place:

The No Lip, No Zip Affair.

This is the safest way to explore your emotional need for extra women. No kissing, no taking any clothes off. Just meet for coffee, spill your guts, tell it all, but refuse to have sex.

The reason I recommend the No Lip, No Zip Affair is there is a strange quirk in our society that says as long as you don't touch her, "nothing happened." You can share the most intimate secrets, reveal yourself in ways you never have with your mate, and as long as you stay zipped, nothing happened.

This will satisfy your need for emotional intimacy without endangering your lifestyle. Your mate may finally object, but a little talk with Miss No Zip will reveal that you've been a perfect gentleman, repeated that you love your wife, and kept everything "clean." If you hear praise for keeping it clean, that will be your hint that your mate thinks sex is dirty.

The No Lip, No Zip Affair is perfect for branching out without getting in too much trouble. Besides, despite popular opinion, part of what you need is just to be around new, exciting females. You don't have to have sex to find this fulfilling. And lucky for you, "nothing happened."

Do you have to be such a boy scout all the time? Hardly. But get comfortable with a low-risk beginning, and you can branch out from there. I know guys who have enviable sex lives because they have learned the ropes gradually, mastering the art of getting their needs met without making themselves vulnerable to the controllers in their lives. It is a process.

So as you graduate from the No Lip, No Zip Affair, evaluate what you are doing like this:

Risk of 1-3. You are starting to reap some rewards, but your risk is rising. Keep your eyes open, reevaluate often, and be ready to bail out at the first hint of danger.

Risk of 4-6. You've gotten pretty adventurous. You may want to shut down your activities for awhile, let everything cool down, be a good boy. Chances are you've got someone wondering what you're up to.

Risk of 7-10. Shut it down now. Way too risky. You are being amateurish, impulsive, and self-destructive.

Only you can decide what you are going to do about this nagging question of whether to have extra women in your life. And you can change your mind as you go along. Just make sure you make your decisions based on what *you* want and what risks you are willing to take on.

The bottom line is if you are watching bottom lines, you're a healthy male. There's nothing wrong with you.

My friendly reminder:

I'm a one-woman man. That's what all my women love about me!

Chapter Two

Extra Money.

Midlife money means more money!

Lots of idiots blow all their money in their midlife crisis. But not you. Even if you've had some losses, have debt, and worry about job security, let's get you covered. You'll come through your midlife crisis with more money and more fond memories than you thought possible.

Oh, I know, people warn that you'll go broke "acting like a kid." They claim to know what's best for you. They mean what's best for them.

Let's set you up so that you finance your midlife crisis without going into debt and without letting anyone else control you. In fact, you're going to be freer than you've ever been. You're not only going to have more money for fun, you're going to have money to invest, and even some to pay off debt if you need to.

No one talks to you about financing your midlife crisis, do they? Has anyone suggested that you open a fun account with enough money to splurge on yourself once in awhile without worry? I didn't think so. Has anyone given you a method for accelerating your investment plan during your midlife crisis? Have they shown you how to enjoy life while reducing debt? Has anyone guided you toward a more fulfilling plan that takes your midlife fears and dreams seriously?

It's not too late, you're not too old, and the people who have underestimated you are in for a big surprise.

If you thought you had to pull back and live less, that's because you're a victim of...

Pack Mule Economics

When did you become a pack mule? Do you feel like a dumb brute with a heavy financial burden strapped on your back while you slog your way down a boring, endless path?

Oh yeah, and if you try to slow down, someone whacks you on the ass with a stick. "We don't have time for you to be tired. Tote that load and quit complaining."

You're a pack mule if you're breaking your back to carry your master's load.

Your master is whoever is in charge of your finances. Let's face it, it's not you. If you had been handling your money like a man instead of a mule, you'd have enough to pursue your dreams, have male fun and even finance your exit from your marriage or job if you want.

But you made some mistakes.

Pack Mule Mistake #1: Making Your Income Your Mate's Business

Ain't love grand? You pledge your heart to another person, and suddenly you're in midlife and someone else thinks they have the right to tell you how to spend your income. That someone is probably benefiting financially from you, and surprise, surprise, that someone may think shopping is a valid use of your money, while having male fun is not.

Think of it like this: someone else is running a business by taking a cut of your income and calling it a relationship. If you don't believe they're in business, try not paying. There'll be more lawyers and accountants involved than you can imagine. It will become perfectly clear that someone thinks your income is their business.

But that's nothing like the marriage between you and the bank.

Pack Mule Mistake #2: Saying "Till Debt Do Us Part"

Debt makes your income the bank's business. If you don't pay on time, they'll make sure they know every dollar you're earning.

Again, just think of not paying, and there'll be lawyers and accountants everywhere.

By the way, if you owe the IRS back taxes, not only is your income their business, they'll publish a notice about the lien they place on you, and now everyone will know your financial status.

Pace Mule Mistake #3: Being a Nice Guy

Hey, you make a little money, you feel generous at home, and next thing you know, there's a whole bunch of redecorating, moving, vacationing and vehicles that are not for you. What a guy! You're such a good provider! Why, just look around. You don't even have a place to set your beer anymore. In fact, beer doesn't really fit in with the new lifestyle, and you shouldn't be drinking anyway. It makes you too tired to earn extra money so there can be a whole bunch more redecorating, moving, vacationing and vehicles that are not for you.

Hey, did you withdraw some money from the account? What was that for? Where did it go? We can't be throwing money away. Don't do that again.

Okay, Mr. Pack Mule, time to think your way out of this. You've got three choices.

1) If you **remain a pack mule**, you will be miserable, then die looking back on a lifetime of regret and drudgery.
2) If you **run or quit**, you will endanger your life. You'll have relief for a while, and then die broke and desperate.
3) But if you **stash away private money**, you'll have enough money to cover your current mess, plus plenty left over for your midlife fun and investing (so you don't get in this mess again).

The pack mule in you may be braying, "Where am I going go get private money? I'm trudging along with my last ounce of energy. And everyone thinks they have a right to every extra dollar I get."

They've sure got you trained. We've got to break out of that pack-mule mentality. Your owners may not realize that while you're in the barn at night, you're not sleeping; you're eyeing that barn door.

Your Exit Strategy.

You've got to exit your wife, life or strife. Something's gotta give.

Your Wife. You may have to face the idea that your wife is draining you financially. Still, I'm not a big fan of divorce in midlife (it messes up your fun) so getting away from your wife may not serve you best right now. But if you feel you have to leave your wife, go to the chapter on divorce and make preparations, so you can come out prosperous.

Your Life. It may be that your lifestyle is the problem. By exiting your life I mean changing your current lifestyle, and downgrading that can be really scary if you don't have a plan. It can feel like failure. Even if you do downsize a bit, I want you to think of it as a temporary strategy, not a permanent change. In fact, you're going to have an even richer life in just a little while. So don't consider some kind of permanent downturn in your lifestyle. It's hard to get rich by cutting back.

Your Strife. Really the long term solution boils down to the third one: let's end the strife. We'll deal with possible divorce and a new life after you've at least had some fun. Your head will be clear then, and you'll have a better idea of what you really want to do once you are not in pain.

So back to arguing with that pack mule. Yes you do have the energy and resources to get some private money. Even in a recession, or if you're in debt, or even if you feel exhausted.

Once you start winning, you'll have more energy than you thought possible. The purpose of a midlife crisis is to improve your life, not wreck it, and when you feel the improvement, when you see a better future for you, you'll have instant energy. I know you're tired, but what the heck, you're used to trudging along, why not trudge along in a prosperous direction?

So let's get real. Here are the actual steps to take to have a prosperous midlife crisis:

Step One.

Cut down the strife in your job. Maybe it's crummy. Maybe you're bored. Maybe you're worried that your age is keeping you from getting promoted. Don't walk off. We're going to make a plan to replace your job, but you've got to do all this in order.

All I want you to do in step one of your exit strategy is to quit causing trouble. Stop arguing with the boss, stop whining about the hours, and stay out of the break room where everybody is complaining. Remember, you don't care. This is just a paycheck. Quit fretting over how things are not running efficiently, stop pointing out management errors. Just keep your head down and smile, because you are making a plan.

And don't brag about that plan, either. Protect yourself. No need in spreading the word that you are on your way to enjoying life instead of trudging along like the rest of them.

Right now, this job is just a way to cover your expenses and help you start your exit strategy.

Step Two

Make a real budget. Not the one your mate approves—the one with a huge "miscellaneous" category you never seem to get to spend. Make this one based on something like this:

Rent/Mortgage

Food

Insurance

Utilities

Debt Service

Midlife Crisis (Fun Account)

Midlife Investing (Freedom Account)

Whoa! Wait! What are those last two items? Fun and investing? For you? How come that never came up during those kitchen table budget discussions? You know the reason, it's because paying for what you want is not in the budget.

Make this budget our little secret. Make the budget you would have if *you* were in charge of your money.

Step Three.

Set an extra money goal. Let's face it, private money for fun is not going to be in the approved budget you share at home. So you're going to need extra.

Don't be afraid. Let's write down the figure, even if you can't see where it's coming from right now.

Hmmm. Fun for you. Money you don't have to account for. Fifty a week? A hundred? More? You tell me. How much would fit your fun expectations?

Now double that. That's right, double. The extra funds will be for your investment strategy.

Here's the top-secret way to keep from going broke during your midlife crisis: invest as much as you "blow."

Whatever amount you spend on your midlife crisis, invest a matching amount. Hey, we're not just working on a good time for now; we want some funds so you can enjoy the rest of your life!

If you want to spend $100 on a night on the town, plan to send $100 to a mutual fund, savings account, money market, etc. If it's $300, you'll send $300. Even if it's twenty bucks, plan to send twenty bucks to your investment fund.

Step Four.

Now let's look at how you're going to get that money.

You have two ways to build wealth: business income and investment growth.

Business income is money you earn by starting a part-time business. Contracting your services on the side, selling magazine articles, consulting, teaching lessons, you get the idea.

It's important that you stop and value who you are and what you can do. In fact, that is the whole point of this book: your value is being overlooked. And sometimes the person doing the overlooking is you yourself. There are things you are good at that people would pay to learn. There may be something you could make, something you could market, something you could distribute that would make you a lot of money.

I can hear the old pack mule now. "I'm not good at anything but working. I don't have any special talents." Aaargh! You are going to make me mad talking like that. Everyone who has survived to middle age is good at lots of things. The only problem is, most have been taught that those things don't count.

Here's an example: A man sells life insurance. That's all he's ever done. No hobbies, nothing else. So how in the heck can he start a business?

Are you kidding? He's already got the primary skill he needs—selling! He sells big ticket stuff, and that's hard to do. I bet he has a natural empathy for people that makes them comfortable with him, and he has the ability to close a sale. It would be very natural for him to start a side business selling something else. He might start selling products or services that make people feel better about their future—since that's basically what he does anyway. So let's say he sells an article called, "The Top Ten Insurance Mistakes Most People Make."

Maybe he's not that good a writer, so he teams up with someone who is. Maybe they create a book together. Or how about if he sells safety equipment for children online? His pitch could be, "In all my years of selling insurance, I have never found any insurance as good as prevention." He could find a supplier for the equipment and basically be the middle man.

Or let's say a guy is an engineer, maybe has a hobby of collecting Civil War miniatures. Not much hope for him, huh?

Oh yeah? What if he wrote a book about engineering during the Civil War? How did they make bridges? How did they blow up bridges? What vehicles, equipment, structures and techniques did they use to move armies and build camps and fortify positions? This guy could become an expert, attending Civil War conventions. He could sell his book, review enthusiasts' miniature constructions for historical accuracy, or become a consultant/display builder for a museum. He could also open an online hobby shop selling supplies for miniature builders. He could also write articles for history magazines—advertising his book at the same time. He could also become an engineering consultant. He could also design and build elaborate playhouses for kids. He could also … see? The ideas just keep flowing once you get the hang of it.

Let's try another one. Let's make it hard. Here's a guy who supervises the janitorial crew for a small hospital. Done it twenty years. Plays guitar badly, spends his evenings watching Wheel of Fortune and crime dramas, and goes grocery shopping with his wife. He's sunk, right?

Wrong. He could start a cleaning service that cleans offices at night and on weekends. He could form a club of bad guitar players, the real purpose of which is to recruit new students for a guitar shop, who would give him a percentage of what he brings in from new student signups. He could invent a game called Crime of Fortune that uses a wheel to determine players' crimes, their fatal flaws, and the qualities of the detective who is on their trail. It could become a murder mystery game people sign up to play at conventions and seminars, or on cruises. He could also start a coupon-clipping service for grocery shoppers. The idea here is that people never have the coupons they need when they want a certain product. But he could keep files of coupons, and be the person you contact to get coupons on specific products. He could make this a membership service, where the customer pays a small fee monthly, with the potential of saving so much money on groceries their membership is effectively free.

Throw another one at me. You're not going to stump me. Everyone has several somethings they are good at. And maybe what you should go into business doing is something you've never done before.

Have you always wanted to ride a motorcycle across the United States? Become a travel agent for motorcycle enthusiasts, planning cool trips for them.

You say your only interests outside of work are naked girls and beer? Form an employment agency for strippers. Require drug tests (at their expense), check references, and interview them for business attitude and work ethic. You get a cut of their first month's salary. In turn they get the safety and convenience of dealing with a nice guy like you who represents them to clubs. The club owners appreciate you because you bring quality girls, and it doesn't cost them anything since your cut comes out of the girls' tips. Or how about offering to sell beer at street fairs for a local bar? You could be their man on the street, not only selling beer, but promoting the bar.

One more: let's say you are a school teacher, math. Your only hobby is gardening. You are tired, stressed, sick of screaming kids. You life is a dud. Hmm. Well first of all, there's something interesting about combining math and gardening. Some of the great gardens of the world included sophisticated mathematical calculations. You could research that. You could turn that research into a teaching gig at a community college. Simple Math Principles for an Award-Winning Garden. Sounds like a book too. Hey, there might be something in Gardening for Teachers: Reduce Stress by Growing Things. You could certainly advertise yourself as a tutor. Or you could become a sales rep for a mathematics book publisher, traveling to educational conventions to push their books.

All these ideas are off the top of my head. There are a lot more buried under the surface. And did you notice that all of them require little or no money to start? You shouldn't go into debt to do this, and you shouldn't risk your life savings. Once you get the knack for inexpensive business startup ideas, you'll be amazed at the opportunities staring you in the face.

If you need help coming up with ideas, get my *Mission Finder* method and work through it until you get a clear picture of who you are and what your talents are. Find something you are good at or interested in and start moonlighting. Form a business entity, and once you have You, Inc. up and running, you'll have great tax write-offs and . . .

Bingo. Fun money. Oh sure, whoever thinks you're a pack mule will expect you to turn over the funds so they can decide what is best for you (and that usually turns out to be more drudgery). But here's what you do. Open your own checking account just for those extra checks—say it's for record-keeping purposes—and just write the household a check from that account. That way, you can keep some for you! Ah! At last. You can make withdrawals without explaining yourself! And you can send some off to an investment account. Success!

Now, is it easy to start a successful business? Who the hell cares if it's hard or easy? You're already suffering. So try. Try hard. Dedicate yourself to finding a business idea you can start with little money, and study on how to do it. Read business startup books on your commute to and from your job. Skip that rerun after the evening news and educate yourself on how to become an entrepreneur. What have you got to lose? You can start with some of the books and links I feature on ManUpMen.wordpress.com and see if these bring the secret entrepreneur in you to life.

If your first business doesn't do that well, scrap it and move on to your second idea. As long as you don't borrow money to start the business, you can afford to have an idea fail. This is your freedom at stake, so don't give up until you find something you can pour yourself into and make some money.

Next start building **investment growth**. This is the best money. It's money that grows on its own.

This kind of growth comes from things like payments from interest and dividends, rents from commercial real estate, or profits from rising stocks.

Investment growth keeps going even if you are not there, and it is the secret of the truly free man. I recommend you start thinking of investments for growth as soon as you get your extra active income going. Remember, you are going to be investing an amount that matches your fun money.

Use this money for dollar-cost averaging. It's a fascinating and simple concept. You invest the same amount of dollars each month in an exchange traded fund, a mutual fund, stock or other investment vehicle.

If the share price has gone down, you get more shares. If the price has gone up, you get fewer shares. Over time, the average share price is all you care about. So let it go up or down, the average cost will be low, and you'll be paying yourself before you pay anyone else. Now that's a change in the right direction!

Every month, before you or anyone else spends your extra checks, you designate a specific amount to be taken out of your checking account and used to purchase shares of a mutual fund, exchange traded fund, stock, REIT, or whatever investment vehicle you decide on. No excuses. You'll be surprised at how you can suddenly invest fifty or a hundred bucks or more just by matching your fun money expenditures.

I realize if your mate investigates or reads your mail, or if she examines your private checkbook, you'll have some explaining to do, because she will assume you're still the old pack mule who only does what you're told, which in this case will mean she thinks you should be turning over all your money for her to budget, instead of making your own investment decisions. So use a cover story. You found this opportunity, and couldn't pass up the chance to protect your family.

Explain dollar cost averaging, promise never to make a decision without permission again, and go to bed happy that you've made a move to get out of pack-mule thinking. Make her the beneficiary on the investment account to cover for the fact that it's not a joint account. Explain that the new checking account is for your side business—just to keep things orderly.

Under this plan, you now have:

Extra money from business income,

Extra money from investment growth,

Money for your own fun.

(For complete details and techniques on how to produce income and growth while keeping your job, get my *How to Finance Your Midlife Crisis Workbook.* By the time you get to the last page, you'll wonder why you ever suffered. Go to www.ManUpMen.wordpress.com to see when it is available.)

Step Five.

Begin your job replacement strategy. Don't stress over it, let's just talk it out.

Relax and enjoy the fact that you are now investing on your own behalf, and have fun money to have that beer or three on the way home.

There are two ways to go on this. Here, have another beer and let's ponder the two ways to get you out of that crummy job. Choose only one of these options. We don't want to kill you; we want to bring you back to life.

First, you could get another job. Get the ol' resume out there and see what happens. Do some networking. In particular, there are meet-up groups just for this purpose. Go to meetup.com and you'll be amazed at the number of groups that meet to help find jobs in your area. (It's also a good way to meet members of the opposite sex... oh never mind, that's another chapter!)

You may think you're too old. You may think you'll never find the same pay or benefits or security somewhere else. But you may be wrong. What the heck. You're already miserable as a pack mule, why not try to convince someone you are a thoroughbred? Worst-case scenario: you keep the job you have now.

The second way to replace your job is to grow that business you started for fun money. Here's the best way to do that. The first year of your new business, set half aside and spend the rest on fun and investing. Keep the original job so all of your new money serves you.

The second year of your new business, as you grow your second income, sock a larger percentage away. Have some fun and do your investing, but save more, like two thirds. Your goal is to get a year's wages saved up. If you grow fast, this can be another year or less. If it takes a little longer, then so be it. At least there is an end to this trail you've been trudging.

Now, when you have a year's salary saved from the business, you can justify devoting yourself fulltime to it and leaving the old job. Quit the job and start working for yourself. That's right, work on the business and grow it so you never end up in this mess again. During the third year, since your expenses are covered by savings, you can sock more away to protect you for the fourth year. Put it in a money market fund or invest in your mutual fund, and your money will make money and you'll be in a position in no time to make the decisions you have longed to make. You'll stop being a pack mule and start being a thoroughbred.

Now if you're saying you don't have money to start a business, let me tell you there are hundreds of business ideas that don't cost much. Start the business as a sideline, and you won't have to invest a bundle. Let it pay for itself as it grows.

I walk you through this step by step in the *How to Finance Your Midlife Crisis Workbook*.

What if you're in debt?

Okay, you like the freedom plan I set out, but you say, "Hey, I'm in debt up to my midlife eyebrows! How am I going to get to a place where I can start a plan to have fun?"

Don't be a pack mule! Your master wants you to keep on trudging. And part of you that is in pain just wants to lie down and quit.

How about a manly choice that's better than either of those? Your debt is all the more reason to start the freedom plan today! Just make a simple adjustment. When you start getting the extra money, use one third for fun, one third for investing, one third to pay off debt.

I mean, come on, you're already paying on the debt, so adding some to it will help you get free sooner. And in the meantime you can enjoy life and build a stash for the future.

Mentally, you'll feel better about paying off the debt when you know you are having some fun and building a future. Most people make the mistake of saying they'll have fun once they are debt-free. This leaves them depressed and demoralized, and makes it less likely they'll have the energy to do the things that will get them out of debt! Don't get grim. Have your fun while you reduce your debt, and build an investment account at the same time. It's a forward-looking, optimistic lifestyle that will do more to get you clear of debt than all the hunkering down and cutting back could ever do.

Don't borrow more money to go into business. You don't need more debt. Use a no-or-low cost idea to get started, and accelerate your income to get yourself free!

What if you're planning to disappear?

Well, cool! Hey, Mr. Secret Agent Man, let's get you the money to do it. You may want to hang on to the job longer, while your side money grows, so you can hide more of it.

Where do you hide it? A lot of people stress over offshore accounts way too early in their disappearance plans. Just put your money in a remote location, but not a secret one. Open an investing account, for example. These accounts link easily to bank accounts and you will have plenty of time to set up a transfer before you take off.

Don't start hiding it now. Just get started stashing it. Then, just before you want to disappear, open that secret account where you will move all the money. That way, the secret account won't be sitting around begging for someone to find it. You'll only have it a short time, just long enough to get your money and run.

Get complete details on hiding money in the soon-to-be published, "Secret Money Places." Watch www.ManUpMen.wordpress.com to see when it comes out. Or put your name in now and we'll tell you when it's out. Read it so you'll know where and when to move your money when your plan springs into action.

Also watch www.ManUpMen.wordpress.com for the publication of *How to Disappear in Midlife* for a complete guide to starting a new life altogether. New everything. New you, new loves, new locale.

There, now don't you feel better? I know you're tired, maybe even scared, but look, since you're already working hard, let's put it toward something that will benefit *you* for a change.

Start today. Make some choices, take some chances. Make your move. Make some plans to enjoy your life.

I hear Tahiti is nice this time of year.

My friendly reminder:

I blow as much as I save, so I'll have another beer to grow my savings!

Chapter Three

Extra Creativity.

Trust your possibilities!

What the hell happened to you? When you were a boy, you could build a fort in the backyard and entertain yourself all summer. You invented adventures in exotic lands, maybe even on undiscovered planets.

You had ideas about all sorts of things you might become. There were so many possibilities!

One reason you may be having a midlife crisis is you've been trained to distrust your possibilities. Along the way someone called your dreams fantasies. And you started believing what they said when you saw what kind of drudgery it takes to maintain a career and pay the bills. Yikes! Life is tough. You have to hunker down and become boring and give up the idea of doing something important, fun and worthwhile. Fun is for other men. Why? Because *someone* in your life needs you to believe that crap.

No wonder you dream of getting away. Someone has robbed you of your adulthood.

I'm picturing a kid watching while his mother makes icing for a cake. He is begging to lick the spoon. Please, please!

Well, as an adult, you get to lick the spoon without asking. You're in charge.

Except when you make someone your new mama, and give her permission to tell you when you can or cannot lick the spoon.

By now you may be so beat up and put down you don't even imagine the spoon anymore. You don't even dream of tasting life and savoring the sweetness.

Now don't tell me you're not the creative type. People who say that think they have to be a painter or writer or musician to be called creative. Here's a secret about creative people: they don't actually create anything. They just combine existing things in new ways.

Way back when, someone put a handle on a bag and voila! A purse. Roller-skating and wrestling combined to make roller derby. And a man examined how cockleburs stick to clothes, and he "created" Velcro.

Every new plant species is the result of cross breeding plants (or genetically altering them). No one actually creates a plant from scratch.

Songwriters borrow from other songs, paintings grow out of previous art movements; buildings share design principles.

Look, you're not going to come up with some creative idea for your life that is completely unrelated to what others have done. You're not looking for some outlandish, never-tried-before strategy for yourself. So don't make the excuse that you can't think of new ideas because you are not creative. You can create plenty. You can create new ways to look at things from another perspective—like what if your MAJOR goal every day was to do something YOU enjoy? Don't tell the boss or the mate that is your goal, they want you subservient and compliant. Your new plan will be our secret. Shhh. Don't let anybody know you have decided to enjoy life. They'll call it a midlife crisis, give you some pills to calm you down, and threaten to take away your livelihood, your home life, and your status.

So keep it to yourself for now. Get your creativity back. Your creativity is simply resourcefulness.

Let's try something. There are two lists below. Combine each element from column one with an element from the other column. Don't just read across the lines horizontally, mix them up. Look at the unusual ideas you get! That's all creativity is—combining things that usually aren't combined.

Write down your new phrases.

A beautiful woman	that gets more important with time
An exotic island	I would do anything to have
A college degree	I'm glad I experienced
A lucrative career	that offers peace of mind
A secret friend	that keeps me going
An old dream	that is good for my spirits
The thing I will never tell	that changed my life
My best mistake	that makes winning seem possible
My greatest hope	that gives me all I really need
That one experience	that's sacred to me
The most amazing vision	that's hard to understand but worth it
The one thing I can change	that seems to be the key

Wow. Here are some phrases I came up with. "A beautiful woman that seems to be the key." "My best mistake I'm glad I experienced." "The most amazing vision that gets more important with time."

These phrases make me think. I suddenly feel that I don't have to be so careful. And I feel that the possibilities are already in my grasp. What is my best mistake and why am I glad I made it? Who is the beautiful woman and what is she the key to? What is my vision, and why is my vision important as I grow?

Write down your new sentences. Each one will be a clue that points you in a new direction. For example, you may have written, "The one thing I will never tell that's sacred to me." Hmm. This sounds like a wonderful secret that could be at the center of your life. Or how about, "A secret friend that keeps me going." Is there someone like that in your life? Do you need someone like that in your life?

Use these new combinations to flex your creative muscles and revitalize your thinking about what your life can be.

Let's get going with the creativity and quit whining about whether you can paint or compose. Use creative ideas to improve your life now. Convert that boring commute into a learning experience with audio books. Find ways to use your coffee and lunch breaks to explore ideas for starting a small business to finance your midlife crisis. Call that old friend after work. You know, the one "that makes winning seem possible," to borrow from our list. All of these will help get new ideas in your head, and when you have new ideas, you can combine them in new ways to change your outlook on life.

Experiment with new ideas, like speaking louder, telling someone what you really think, walking differently, dressing better, growing a beard, joining a club, starting a club, advertising yourself, changing your name, wearing a hat, turning left instead of right on your way home and getting up early to write down something new you are going to try today.

Creativity is about doing the unexpected. Surprise yourself. Win someone's disapproval. Make some waves.

Be bad. Write that bad poem, plant that bad garden; take a course and do badly at it. What the hell. You don't have to be the best at everything. Join a pottery group and build a monstrosity. Put it in your living room, and if someone criticizes it, ask, "Where is *your* creation?" At least you did it.

Be a doer, not a dreamer.

Look, I'm not fooling around here. I don't want you to just think about changing things, I want you to really do it. Now. Today. Change one thing. Just one. I dare you.

So let's get real about this. I want you to complete the following sentences.

1. Today I will do something I've never done before, which is …
2. I am going to look at mistakes I've made, and see them as something I did right by seeing myself as …
3. One way I've never thought of to make money is …
4. Women would treat me differently if I just believed that I …
5. A fun thing I haven't done in too long is …
6. Something I've never tried that sounds fun is …
7. If I really focused and believed in myself, I could …
8. The lifestyle that really fits me is …
9. If I spent ninety days doing _____, it would change my life.
10. If my life up to now were a novel, here is how the second half would surprise readers:

Okay, you get the idea. Use those ten sentences as thought-starters. Write ten more of your own. You don't have to have all the answers, just ask some fantastic questions.

Write "What if …" on a piece of paper ten times, and complete it ten different ways.

List the three things you hate about your life and imagine ways to get rid of them. Be wild with your strategies. It's only words. You can crumple up the paper later.

I'll tell you another secret about creativity. Those ideas that you think are so crazy usually feel kind of tame once you really do them. No big deal. Makes you wonder why you didn't try it before. Lots of people have probably done the things you are afraid to try. They survived. What are you afraid of?

Let's talk about something no one ever mentions when they talk about midlife crisis. Sometimes you feel bad, not because you haven't done what you set out to do, but because you HAVE done what you set out to do. You did it. You got married, had kids, got a good job, and lived the American Dream. Only now it seems kind of dull.

You may need a jolt of creativity just to imagine an enjoyable way to spend all those years that lie ahead of you, teasing you like a pretty girl with a sly smile. What are the possibilities? You've never thought of yourself as anything but what you are now, and you are stumped, but excited. So come on, cowboy, pilot, playboy, mountain climber, entrepreneur, lion tamer, house painter, yacht salesman. Imagine something you never even considered doing.

My friendly reminder:

I'm going to surprise everybody, including myself!

Chapter Four

Extra Fun.

Have some boy toys and man trips!

Fun. Toys. Adventure. These are the things people really ridicule you for during a midlife crisis. It's like there's a fun bank and only kids get to make withdrawals. None for you, there's not enough.

We're not going to put up with this. You're going to have some fun, some toys and some adventures that don't break the bank or threaten your marriage. Unless you're married to someone who thinks fun is for her and not you. In that case, keep your fun to yourself, and leave her to wonder why you don't talk to her anymore.

Toys

So first let's get to toys. Motorcycles. Cars. Boats. Guitars. Video Games. Anything you want. Hey, that's a new one, something *you* want. Not something sensible or something someone else approves of for you, but something you enjoy.

I can just hear your critics. "Ah oh, there he goes, blowing all his money on boy toys. Tsk, tsk. And there's poor Jane at home trying to budget their *real* needs, like shopping, jewelry, knick knacks, and trips for her."

What you want is frivolous, even if it's your money. Good. Let's be frivolous. That's pretty much the definition of fun.

Did I say go broke? I don't think so. There are ways to have your toys and keep your savings. Besides, for every dollar you spend on toys, you are going to invest a matching dollar.

Let's say you are just dying to get out on the open road on a Harley. Did you know they have a rental program? Yeah, you can be out there this afternoon without qualifying for a loan and promising your left nut to pay it off. The same goes for fast cars (and fast women, but we won't go there), as well as cool gear for music, video games—you can rent everything from Winnebagos to airplanes.

Yeah, it's not the same as owning, I get it. But here's the deal. What if you don't love it? What if you do love it, but don't want to do it every day? Why be tied to it financially when you're not using it?

Go have your fun and see if you love it. If you do, you can always buy later. Don't bet the farm on one toy. Heck, if you hang on to your money, you can enjoy all the toys you want to, and not have any payments.

Besides, you won't have to park it at the house and endure all the mockery from your significant bother. I mean other.

But what if it's something like a compound bow or a high-tech camera you can't rent? And what if you really, really want to own one?

All right, you know the drill. Get your money together, and buy your toy, while investing an equal amount. If you will make payments, make an equal payment to your mutual fund or investment fund.

Those are the rules. I'm not going to see you go broke like an adolescent wild child just because you want to play. If you can't afford to invest as much as you blow, don't blow any. You'll thank me later. If you wait until you can afford both the toy and the matching investment, you'll have your toys and your security, and instead of being a fool they can mock, you'll be this really smart guy who knows how to live it up.

Adventures

Paris, Tahiti, a tour of the world's nude beaches. Whatever travel destination you dream of, the reason you've never gone may have something to do with not having permission from your owner. I mean your one true love.

Do you ever go on vacation and feel like you're watching everyone else have a good time? You are paying to do something that isn't for you, in the name of "family time" or "togetherness." Okay, good for you, Mr. Togetherness.

You may need to indulge Mr. Aloneness a little bit. Hey, is that the phone ringing? What? You have to go out of town for your new business—the one you started after you read the Extra Money chapter? Damn. That's going to take you away from home.

Or maybe you just won't tell anyone where you're going. You're going to be gone for awhile, and that's it. Call it hunting (hey maybe it *is* hunting), call it sanity time, call it your desire to "get some space." Whatever you need to do to go to the places that are about you and what you want. You're not always going to be selfish about vacations, but this one is all yours, and dammit, you're not going to explain it until you're blue in the face. It's not you're fault the Tiki bar where you're going features topless girls. You had no way of knowing.

Oh, the direct approach isn't realistic in your household? Go on a double vacation. That's when you go to a place and your wife thinks she is having one vacation, while in reality you are having another. You arrive at the hotel and unpack, and she wants a nap. You decide to go for a walk. Just so happens that walk takes you past the Flying Jock Strap Bar and Grill, world-renowned for its two-dollar beer and fatal lap dances. Hey, it may also take you past the historic district, which you really wanted to see but your mate thought would be a drag.

The point is, whatever your interests, why give them up just because your handler doesn't approve or want to participate? I mean, not your handler, your Sweet Little Valentine.

Go on a double vacation by researching your destination before the trip. Every location in the world has a second attraction, the one guys like you really want to see while the wife is off looking at the folk dancers and the crocheted doilies in the shape of her favorite country star.

What we're NOT going to settle for is you being one of those hunch-shouldered wimps carrying his wife's purse and switching his weight from one foot to the other while she tries on sun dresses. I mean, come on, you're a man, not a purse holder. Let's let her stand around waiting while you check out the female bartenders at Willie's Wicked Ways. Yeah, that'll happen. You'll be better off just keeping your excursions to yourself.

Try a double vacation. It takes some James Bond moves to pull it off, but that adds to the fun, and you can at least feel the testosterone surging when you make an effort to do man stuff.

Hooky Hotel

You don't have to go out of town to have fun. This one is fantastic. Take the day off work but don't mention it at home. Go to a hotel. I'm not talking hookers and debauchery, I'm saying have some pizza and beer and watch TV and do what the hell you want, including throwing your underwear on the floor and leaving food on the nightstand. Just be a guy for a day.

Saturday Slip Away

Can't afford the hotel? Wifey won't allow the expense? All right, how about a Saturday alone? You can go out and just do what you want. Stroll around the park, go to the golf shop, go see that movie the two of you couldn't agree on. So without money as an excuse, what's the reason you aren't having some Saturdays or other days to yourself? It's because you're not allowed, let's face it. Maybe, just maybe, you can squeeze in a day to yourself if she is busy. You might not be able to explain how you could possibly go enjoy yourself when there are so many fix-it jobs to do around the house. Here's an explanation: you have the same freedom she does.

Mate Date

Okay, let's include her. Ask her out. But only for fun. No errands, no shopping. Just a fun, footloose day together playing. You won't be able to do *everything* you might do alone, but that's okay, fun is fun. Try it. If you find out she can't do it, that she just has to have some errand or purpose to the trip, you'll know you're back to your own ideas. But she won't be able to say you never want to do anything with her. All she'll be able to say is she doesn't want to have fun with you. If it *does* work, you have it made. You have togetherness, that free feeling, and some relief from the suspicion that your relationship is a job.

Man Trips

No matter how much fun you have with your mate, you still are going to want some man trips. Hunting, fishing, race car driving, a tour of the *Best Sports Bars of All Time* (watch for the book @ www.ManUpMen.wordpress.com).

Whatever the destination, you deserve some time away with the guys. And you shouldn't have to give a detailed report when you get back. From whitewater rafting to deep sea fishing, there are just some things guys do better together. You can cuss like a sailor, drink what you want, and well, just quit being careful.

Don't you hate thinking about everything you say before you say it? Guys just blurt out what's on their minds, and if someone says something truly offensive, everyone just pours beer on his head and tells him he's a nut. Gaffe over. It's fun, easy, and carefree.

You gotta get some man trips. "But what am I going to do while you're gone?" she may ask. Well, a girl trip! What's wrong with that? Suggest it, and you'll show that you're not trying to keep her from doing things that are good for her. Long pause. It will suddenly dawn on her that she is trying to keep you from doing things that are good for you.

If you have to explain it too much, just sneak off on a "business" trip and don't tell her. Some women just insist on being lied to.

Hobbies and Sports

Do you love stuffed deer heads more than you love your mate? Would you rather build a ship in a bottle than build a relationship? Of course not. It's just plain weird that women get jealous of men's hobbies.

So you tinker with old cars. So like to mount fish on plaques and hang them on the wall. If you give up your activities just because your mate objects, then you are giving up your hobby for her hobby of castrating you and hanging your balls in her trophy case. This one is non-negotiable. You deserve to have your interests. They are yours, and no one else has the right to approve or disapprove.

Suggest relationship counseling, and she'll back down. She'll realize how unhealthy it is to demand that you give up being who you are, and she won't want a stranger to know about it.

The same goes for your sports. Dammit, this is your health and well-being. Golf, tennis, running, softball, just plain exercise, whatever. Don't you dare get old and flabby watching Wheel of Fortune and wishing you could get out of the living room and get some fresh air. And if you already are flabby, well all the more reason to get moving.

Now I mean it. You are going to have to confront this one head on. No divorce judge in the world would go against you for wanting to get out in the sunshine and play once in awhile. Make your stand. You owe it to all of us guys.

Take a Course

If you've always wanted to learn how to tie flies or build wooden toys or learn how to unhook a bra with one hand, there is a course or a group to teach you to do it. Go to Craigslist or Meetup.com and find it.

There is no way to be depressed when you are learning something. There is no way you can be defeated if you always pursue your passions. You should always be learning, expanding, growing your brain connections. Take a class.

Oh you're not allowed? How can you take an evening away from your home and family? Here's how: sign up, pay for it, then announce it. Too late to object now. It would just be a waste of money. Besides, you told them you were coming. Gosh, Honey, I wasn't thinking. Oh well, I'll just have to tough it out. Oh by the way, we're all going out for drinks after class.

Hey, while you are squeezing in classes, take a class on how to improve, whether it's dressing better, talking to women or learning how to handle your money better. I'm telling you, you are going to write and thank me. It will change your life. And ultimately, it will win the respect of your mate if you make a stand for your own self-improvement.

Live Now.

Maybe you're saving your money, and maybe your relationship needs work. Maybe there are things that need fixing around the house. But you also have to live. Put some fun back into your life. When did things get so grim?

Come on, you don't have to justify this one. Or if you do have to justify it, Google "Recreation and Mental Health" and print out an article and leave it on the kitchen table. Hell, frame it and put it over the sofa.

If this is a male issue in your house, if the idea is that what guys want to do for fun is unacceptable and has to be approved, then you are living under a death sentence. Someone is being a tyrant and trying to make it sound like you have a flaw, when all you have is a natural human urge to move, learn and enjoy.

Don't let someone take all the fun out of your fun. They'll take the life out of your life.

My friendly reminder:

I don't have

fantasies,

just things to do.

Chapter Five

Extra Health.

Get in shape for greatness!

You don't just need to be in shape, you need to get tough.

There are lots of mamby-pamby diets and exercise programs that were designed for women and then adjusted for men as an afterthought.

You're not an afterthought.

You're a tough guy. Maybe you've been temporarily beaten down, but you know you're really a tough guy. You can't survive to middle age without being a tough guy. Everything up to now has been practice for becoming a full-blown man.

So you need a health plan to bring out the tough guy that's hiding inside. Let's get you on a path to be the best you've ever been. Not just a little better, but your best.

One of the things that will anger you the most is when people tell you midlife is the beginning of declining health. They'll give you adult diapers for your birthday and think they're being cute. Ha ha. They laugh and pat you on the back when they give you that "over the hill" card. Jerks.

I sincerely hope you have done *something* in your misguided youth that you're paying for. Life's no fun if you're too careful. But there's no reason to expect a sad decline in your health. In fact, you could get in the best shape of your life. You could eat foods that energize you and help you live up to your capacity. .

Look at it this way: whatever your health is now, you can improve it.

All right, let's get down to one of the main barriers to better health in a midlife crisis. How are you going to do everything from drinking, dining and staying out late while exercising, eating better and taking care of your health?

You deserve to party if you want to. Just don't do it every night. Space things out. Train for you binges. Get in shape before you party, and you'll party better. Then allow for some resting and recuperating time after you party, and you can start all over again.

Don't feel like you have to keep up with some young girl's nightlife just to keep her. Why do you have to keep her? There are plenty of girls out there. Play hard to get. Don't be so available. You are a busy, successful man who has a lot of things to do. Maybe she'll respect you more if you don't let her lead you into a lifestyle. Haven't you had enough of being led around already? Think of it as being in training for a life of wine, women and song. Don't be one of those sad cases who sacrifice their health for the party life. You'll have a longer party if you take care of yourself on non-party days.

Another way to juggle your debauchery with your health kick is to save the wild stuff for your travel dates. You'll look like a model for self-improvement at home, and you'll be the poster boy for fun and adventure while you're away.

Okay, so we're agreed. You're going to have your wild times and improve your health.

So go see your doctor to check out any problems, and if you get the go-ahead, take a look at the Man-Up Men Exercise and Diet Regimen. Even if you're in good shape, you can improve *something*. And if you're not in good shape, just a little effort will prepare you for the adventures that lie ahead.

Let's do some man-sized thinking about a new approach to your health.

The Man-Up Men Exercise and Diet Regimen

The Get-Even Workout. If you try to get in shape just because someone says you should, you'll just quit. You've been bossed around enough. It never works.

Here's a better reason to work out: to get even with all the assholes that have put you down and held you back. That's right. Get even. Forget that "forgive and forget" crap. John F. Kennedy said, "Forgive your enemies, but never forget their names."

I say why waste all that energy even forgiving, when you could use that energy to make yourself stronger?

A get-even workout is tougher, meaner and more powerful than a get-in-shape workout. Here's how to start:

Knock 'Em Out. Visualize one of the people who have cut you down or held you back. Imagine their image right in front of you. Now throw a punch. You can't be a wimp after punching someone out.

Don't worry, we won't really beat anyone up. We'll sue them or get even in a less risky way. But for now, use them to energize your workout.

Throw straight punches, ten per arm.

Place your fists palm-up at your hips and alternate punches as you twist your fist over. Ten per arm.

Do uppercuts. Ten per arm.

Pound down on their heads. Ten per arm.

Elbow jabs. Look out, they're behind you. Do ten.

Boxing style. Get in your best stance and give 'em jabs and roundhouse punches.

Forward kicks. Snap your foot up into their groins. Ten per leg.

Side kicks. Good for balance. Jab your flat foot to the side and take down those jerks who are trying to get around you.

Kick back. Watch your balance again. They're behind you. Get 'em.

Outlast the Bastards. This is your stamina portion of the workout, more aerobic. The idea here is to thwart all the people who said you'd never last. We'll show 'em.

Walk/Run with a visual goal. Choose either walking or running based on what shape you're in. You should be able to talk comfortably while you're moving. If you are wheezing, you're going too fast.

Get a visual goal—a stop sign or a place on the track you are going to make it to. When you get to it, raise your fists in the air. Celebrate reaching your goal. If you need to go around one more time, celebrate that time too. And they said you couldn't do it. Do this three to five times a week.

Do just enough to feel energized, not exhausted.

Screw 'Em. Do sexual exercises. They're called Kegels, named after some guy who thought of them. These will help prevent premature ejaculation and will help give you control and strength. Here's how you do them. Identify the muscles involved in stopping your urine flow in midstream. Feel it? Okay, now how would you restart the flow? Feel that? Those are the two exercises (without the peeing, of course).

> **Kegels.** Sit down with your feet together and your knees sticking to the sides.
> **Do the lifts** you identified when stopping the flow. Start with 15 and work your way up to 100 with time.
> **Do the restart motion.** Move from 15 reps to 100.
> **Now do the first one again, but hold it** for 15 to 20 seconds.
> **Do the second one and hold it too.**

What you visualize while you do this is your business. But make it enjoyable. Whoever you are visualizing, you should look forward to doing your Kegel exercises more than any other part of your workout.

By the way, there's no substitute for the real thing. Make sex part of your sex workout! Tell her it's a health requirement.

Testosterone Diet. There's nothing like the roar of testosterone in your veins to make you stand up to the people who try to frighten you into submission.

Scare 'em right back with your newfound power. Eat foods that boost your testosterone and you'll feel like a giant stomping past the piss ants.

Think Zinc. In trials, it helped raise testosterone and sperm levels. Try a supplement.

Oysters. Hey, surprise. They contain zinc.

Eat Meat. Steaks, ribs, roast, pork and chicken contain zinc.

Beans. They'll boost your man hormones.

Whole Grains. You guessed it, zinc.

Dairy Products. Milk, cottage cheese and yogurt will give your balls a boost too.

Eggs. And keep the yolks. Testosterone is made from cholesterol.

Broccoli. Here's a surprise. It helps reduce estrogen. You don't need more estrogen controlling your life do you?

Cabbage. Works like broccoli.

Nuts. They'll help reduce your risk of coronary disease.

Garlic. It'll not only boost your testosterone, it will keep Vampiresses away.

Tribulus Terrestris. Sorry for throwing a Latin name at you. It's also called Puncture Vine, Caltrop, Yellow Vine, and Goathead, and sometimes gokshura. Some claim it boosts testosterone. It comes as a supplement. It's an herb.

Magnesium. Make sure you're getting this too. It's good for growing muscle, which boosts testosterone.

Cut out Sugar. It lowers testosterone and reduces your sex drive.

I'm not going to bombard you with portions and milligrams on these.

You're a big boy, just add these to your diet and you'll be roaring in no time. Hey, you're going to eat anyway, might as well eat manly stuff.

Outsmart 'Em. Don't ignore your mind. It needs exercise just like the rest of you does. There are a whole bunch of boring studies that come to the not-so-boring conclusion that exercising your brain is just like exercising muscles. Your mind gets stronger with use. If you don't want to end up some drooling idiot in Bermuda shorts and colored socks who can't remember where he put his keys, you better learn often and learn well, and keep your mind nimble. Treat your mental workout as seriously as you do your physical workout.

Memory. Every time you make a list, memorize it. Even if you have to go back to the list eventually, the practice will do you good. So at least when you are sent to the store for milk, bread, eggs and tampons, you can remember the first three.

Problem Solving. Not necessarily math problems. Get out pencil and paper and figure things out. Write it out, draw it, solve a dilemma. It will make you smarter by relying on your own brain instead of waiting for someone else to hand you answers. Here's one to get you started: What are all the advantages a middle-aged man has over a younger man?

Perceiving Details. When you have to wait on someone, spend your time noticing details around you. How many people are wearing black shoes? How many have on ties? What geometric patterns are in the décor? Picking out details is a huge skill, and practice will make you sharper.

Language. Get a book on vocabulary building and learn a word a day. Some desk calendars are designed for this, too. You'll make new brain connections that will last you a lifetime. Do crossword puzzles. Write a journal (don't put anything incriminating in it).

Listening. I know, she says you never listen, and that makes you want to quit listening. But practice it for yourself. Spend an hour every once in awhile just listening to what's going on around you. It really boosts your brain and your sense of being alive.

Reaction Time. Make up games to challenge your reflexes. Like the next time the phone rings, you have to have to grab it as fast as you can. Set an alarm for a few minutes ahead, and pick something up off the table as soon as the alarm goes off. Stay fast. It could save your life and it will keep you young.

Math. Every so often, put the calculator away and come up with the total for yourself. Divide, multiply. Figure percentages. Don't tell me you were never good at math. This is a workout, no excuses.

Emotional Workout. That's right, work on getting tougher emotionally. You need to be in charge of your emotions instead of letting someone else push your buttons. That's what this whole book is about. I want you to do several things for your emotional health.

Choose How You Feel. I mean it. You decide which emotions will serve you best in a situation, and decide to feel that way. Is it better to feel angry or powerful when someone tells you that you're a failure? Powerful works better. Well, then, dredge up an image or phrase that reminds you that you're powerful. Would it be best to feel like you're falling in love with the secretary? No. It will jeopardize your job. So put those lovey dovey feelings away and feel like a professional. This is the hallmark of a man: he chooses emotions that help him win.

See Someone about Your Depression. Don't let them talk you out of your midlife crisis plan, but find someone who will let you clear your head and get focused on having some fun and winning some battles. Just be aware of two things:
1) Female counselors may have a tendency to disapprove of your midlife crisis plan—even if they are extremely

professional, their assumptions about what is healthy and positive may not match what you want;

2) If you tell a mental health professional about any illegal activities, they *may* be required to break confidentiality and report it.

Reduce that Stress. There are several ways. More exercise. Deep breaths. More sex. More laughter. More alone time. Vacations and hooky days. In other words, put your well-being first and quit people-pleasing, and you'll have a lot less stress in your life. And replace that awful job. Oh yeah, I almost forgot. Eliminate shopping. Tell her I said it's medically necessary.

Take Sam-e and Vitamin B. That first one is a supplement. It's a little pricey, but it's cheaper than therapy. In fact, many therapists are using it. This is a knockout combination that will help you feel terrific. You'll have a better outlook and you might even sing a song on your way to work.

Don't Get Mad, Get Even. Find ways to pay back people who do you wrong. It's good for you. You'll quit feeling like a victim and start acting like a winner. There's nothing better for you emotionally than feeling like a winner. Winners don't let wrongs go unanswered.

Every one of these ideas, including more sex, will make you healthier automatically. I know you're at the time of your life when you want to indulge, and I'm all for it. I'm just saying with a little health awareness you can indulge longer! There's no reason your midlife crisis has to be an irresponsible descent into self-destruction. You're not dismantling yourself; you're reinventing yourself. You can reinvent a healthy, wealthy, robust man if you want.

So exercise, eat right, sleep well, party, recuperate and stay in balance.

Oh yeah, a word about sexual health. High-risk sexual activities are for self-destructive wimps. Respect yourself. Use condoms, avoid skanks, and don't make your sexual decisions while drunk or overexcited.

Foster a life wish, not a death wish. You wouldn't dive off a high rise without a parachute, so why dive into a sex affair without protection?

One other thing to remember regarding your health is that you *may* come out of your midlife experimentation wanting what you had. You don't want to be pitiful if you want your mate to take you back or keep you. Stay healthy. Improve. Go into the next phase as the healthiest you possible.

Oh, and another thing. Keep that health insurance premium paid! Don't be a putz and throw away health insurance. If you get something like cancer or need to be hospitalized, you can come out of it and get back to having fun. You won't be bankrupt, and you'll get good health care. Don't jeopardize your health by being stupid. Remember, your midlife crisis is not an adolescent rebellion; it's a mature decision to live better.

Another professional you may want to see is a urologist to get some hard-on pills. In fact, you can get your physical with this person and kill two birds with one exam. It's common for men to feel silly seeking medicine to restore erections, but there's something you should know.

Many medical experts suggest that if you don't keep the ol' blood pumping down there, you may lose function altogether. Yikes! If you need chemical help, don't let anyone shame you into destroying your sex life for the rest of your life!

Your entire quest for health during your midlife crisis may be blocked by naysayers and people who don't care if you get better. You are allowed to discover what is healthy for you. Educate yourself about your options for a healthier, more vigorous lifestyle. You don't have to go crazy to go wild.

Also, be aware that building muscle boosts testosterone. So if you decide to start working out with weights, please get a personal trainer. A trainer can help prevent you from getting hurt when you take on free weights or weight machines.

Now get out there and live more of your life! Today!

My friendly reminder:

I <u>might</u> forgive,

but I <u>never</u> forget!

Chapter Six

Extra Commitments for Your Marriage.

<u>Your</u> commitments are only half the equation!

Women want to talk about commitment--from you, not them. The usual "commitment conversation" centers on the assumption that you are commitment-phobic. Poor misguided fool. You just haven't grown up yet. You don't understand commitment like women do. But lucky you, they are willing to train you.

Well gosh, thanks. But no thanks. You're no fool. You just happen to understand that *your* commitments are one side of the coin. Her commitments are the flip side. So, Dear Ms. Commitment, let's have a midlife commitment conversation.

Midlife Marriage Commitments

1. Dreams. One of the purposes of marriage is to help make my dreams come true. You hereby recognize your commitment to

being supportive of my dreams and not using marriage as an excuse to destroy my hopes and desires. You won't complain about my dreams, and you won't begrudge me the time and money I spend pursuing what I really want.

2. Debt. Debt is the enemy of prosperity. You agree not to use credit cards to shop for anything we can't pay for in the same month. You further agree to help make us debt free by applying any extra money we have to paying off credit cards before any more shopping takes place.

3. Self-esteem. Marriage should help build self-esteem. You agree that put-downs are not appropriate when talking to me. You agree that you will help me focus on my strengths without mocking my weaknesses.

4. Alone time. Separate activities are healthy. You agree not to coerce me into activities that I don't enjoy by pretending that is part of commitment. Because you respect me as an individual, you understand there will be times you want to do something that I don't, and this doesn't reflect on my commitment level.

5. Personal cash. You agree that we will each have our own money to spend as we wish, without justification, explanation or aggravation.

6. You agree not to castrate me. In fact, one of the things you like about me is I like women. I appreciate femininity, including yours! You understand that I will always notice women, and you will not ask me to lie about it.

7. Earning money. You agree that I don't work for you. We run a household together, and I am committed to supporting that, but I don't turn over my income for you to manage. You recognize that

my ideas for spending, saving, investing and splurging are just as valid as yours.

8. Extras. It is fun to splurge, but you agree that we will invest as much as we blow.
9. Guy time. You agree that it is healthy for me to have male friends. You will not protest when I want to go out with the guys. You will not grill me when I get home.
10. Financial meanness. You agree that you don't want to ruin me financially. In the event things don't work out between us, you agree not to try to take all our assets. In fact, you agree to the following lists:

My assets	Your assets
_____	_____
_____	_____
_____	_____
_____	_____
_____	_____
_____	_____
_____	_____
_____	_____
_____	_____
_____	_____
_____	_____
_____	_____

11. Custody. Our children are our children. Not yours, not mine. Joint custody is the only option for us, if for any reason we don't make it as a couple.

Signed _____

Signed _____

Date _____

Leave that on the kitchen table, and you'll have a good idea whether you are in an equal marriage. Yes, she will have a great point if she says she should have the same kind of agreement written for her. Excellent. She has agreed to equality!

Whip this out:

Midlife Marriage Commitments
From the Husband to
The Wife

1. Dreams. One of the purposes of marriage is to help make my dreams come true. You hereby recognize your commitment to being supportive of my dreams and not using marriage as an excuse to destroy my hopes and desires. You won't complain about my dreams, and you won't begrudge me the time and money I spend pursuing what I really want.
2. Debt. Debt is the enemy of prosperity. You agree not to use credit cards to shop for anything we can't pay for in the same month. You further agree to help make us debt free by applying

any extra money we have to paying off credit cards before any more shopping takes place.

3. Self-esteem. Marriage should help build self-esteem. You agree that put-downs are not appropriate when talking to me. You agree that you will help me focus on my strengths without mocking my weaknesses.

4. Alone time. Separate activities are healthy. You agree not to coerce me into activities that I don't enjoy by pretending that is part of commitment. Because you respect me as an individual, you understand there will be times you want to do something that I don't, and this doesn't reflect on my commitment level.

5. Personal cash. You agree that we will each have our own money to spend as we wish, without justification, explanation or aggravation.

6. You agree not to shut me down. In fact, one of the things you like about me is I like men. I appreciate masculinity, including yours! You understand that I will always notice men, and you will not ask me to lie about it.

7. Earning money. You agree that I don't work for you. We run a household together, and I am committed to supporting that, but I don't turn over my income for you to manage. You recognize that my ideas for spending, saving, investing and splurging are just as valid as yours.

8. Extras. It is fun to splurge, but you agree that we will invest as much as we blow.

9. Girl time. You agree that it is healthy for me to have female friends. You will not protest when I want to go out with the girls. You will not grill me when I get home.

10. Financial meanness. You agree that you don't want to ruin me financially. In the event things don't work out between us, you agree not to try to take all our assets. In fact, you agree to the following lists:

My assets   Your assets

_____   _____
_____   _____
_____   _____
_____   _____
_____   _____
_____   _____
_____   _____
_____   _____
_____   _____
_____   _____
_____   _____

11. Custody. Our children are our children. Not yours, not mine. Joint custody is the only option for us, if for any reason we don't make it as a couple.

Signed _____

Signed _____

Date _____

These agreements will lead to some great discussions about what your marriage is for. Why are you both in it? What are your expectations? Sadly, most people discuss these things before the wedding, but seldom revisit them in mid-marriage.

You both are changing. In fact, you're having a midlife crisis. Adjust your marriage to your changing needs.

I know, it takes some balls to slap such an agreement on the table, but it beats divorce. When it comes to marriage, grow a pair and make it fair.

My friendly reminder:

Sure I'm committed! I'm committed to my well-being! Are you?

Chapter Seven

Extra Divorce Protection.

Have a great divorce that benefits you!

There are good reasons to get a divorce. And there are good ways to get a divorce. But you have to be aware that getting divorced during your midlife crisis will make it less fun. Most of the benefits you imagine are on the far side of a lot of turmoil and stress, even if your divorce goes smoothly.

Still, it can be a good move. During a midlife crisis, you are deciding how you want to live the rest of your life. One of the reasons you may be in crisis is that your marriage is a disappointment. Here are some reasons to get a divorce.

She's Showing Signs of Sock-drawer Jowl. You've seen those old couples. He is hunch-shouldered. She is frowning, with her jowls hanging, dragging her mouth and demeanor down, down, down.

They got this way through years of nagging. She has been peering into his sock drawer and complaining that it's a mess for decades. Of course, it's not just his sock drawer. It's his desk, his shoes in the closet, his car. Nothing has ever been neat enough, good enough.

Her heavy perfectionism has weighed down his shoulders and pulled her jowls into a permanent frown.

Midlife is an excellent time to decide if you want to wake up in a few years and find you are married to an old woman with sock-drawer jowl.

You Married a Sex Shifter. Remember when she liked sex? I don't mean lovemaking, I mean sex. She was adventurous, naughty, lusty and fun. Then she started watching talk shows and decided sex was about love. And not just some of the time, all of the time. It has to be lovemaking all the time. Tender, slow, gentle, considerate. Boring.

Next thing you know, she started ridiculing "bimbos" in bikinis. Look at them parading everything for all the world to see. Isn't that just disgusting? Yes, you say. It certainly is. What a shame. All those boobs and butts you have to look at.

Yawn. If you married a sex shifter, one who changed the sex rules on you, then you may want to ask yourself if you can stand a half-lifetime of lovemaking without relief. You'll have to lie to her while lovemaking, never letting her know that you're getting through the lovemaking by imagining bimbos in bikinis.

You're Left Holding the Purse. Do you want to be one of those guys in the dress department, shuffling his feet and trying to look like the purse he is holding is *definitely* not his? Guys have a way of holding their wives' purses that says, "Hey, this is awkward. I don't carry a purse. To prove it, I can't even figure out which way you hold this. I know, I'll tuck it like a football."

At some point in many marriages, the wife decides the man's job is to go shopping with her. He becomes her shopping buddy. She measures the relationship by how much he complains about shopping. Message: shut up and stand there while I try on seventeen dresses and then buy the one you hate.

Of course, she makes it fair by going with you to the sports bar and tossing back some suds while cheering on your team. Yeah right. Never happen.

If your dates start and end at the shopping mall, you may have to face the fact that you've become a purse holder. Do you want to die a purse holder? Have you been imagining handles on the football during games? You might need emergency action. And if that purse you're hugging holds your paycheck, you are in big trouble.

Your Lips are as Buttoned as Your Fly. Does she "shush" you a lot? Do you have to get approval for your opinions? Does she often comment, "I can't believe you said that"? Have you just quit saying things because you know she'll disapprove?

Have you noticed she speaks freely?

And have you noticed you are not in the mood for sex lately?

That's because you are all buttoned up. Freedom to express yourself is a right, not a privilege. If you are asking permission to speak, you are asking permission to live.

You will end up an old man with his lips clamped together and balls the size of peanuts, who thinks kids are too loud and who says people should keep their opinions to themselves. You'll be allergic to exuberance, free expression and joy.

You Plan to Live a Long Life. Maybe you've had a good or okay marriage. Maybe you're just through being married. You have a lot of life left to live, and you want to try something else.

Maybe you even love her. But it's time to live the rest of your life, and you don't want to be half a couple anymore.

If you want to travel light, experiment with your life, and even do things that are not approved of in your marriage, that does not make you an asshole. It just means you have outgrown your marriage.

Hey, a lifetime used to be forty or fifty years. People live longer now. You could have a whole lifetime people didn't get generations ago. You may have been a good husband, father, provider and all around good guy for a lifetime already, and now it's time for your second lifetime. It's a legitimate reason to move on.

The Worst Reason to Get a Divorce. You met someone else. You're in love with her. You want to spend all your time with her. What a lousy reason to get a divorce.

You are becoming a serial monogamist. One owner after another. Oh, but she's not like that. Uh huh.

Look, even if she's wonderful, you can't move from one marriage to another and remain sane. You have to get out on your own, make some fresh decisions, make some fresh mistakes, and get your bearings.

Even if your new love is wonderful, she deserves a man who knows how to stand on his own. She deserves a guy who is not needy. If you need her, you are not a full grown man. Grow up first. Then see if you want her when you no longer need her.

Your Divorce Plan

So, you decide if you have good reasons for a divorce. But you don't have to lose out. There are many things you can do to plan for your divorce so you can protect yourself and get on with being free. YOU NEED A PLAN. There's nothing wrong with planning your divorce instead of reacting when it hits you. Don't get caught without a life while she goes on and lives hers.

You *must* take several steps in advance. If the "d" word has even been mentioned in your house, don't be an idiot. Move into action mode now. Here are your action steps:

Shut up. This is step one. Stop telling her how you feel, insisting on expressing your emotions and making your stands. They're not suddenly going to matter just because you keep saying they should. All you are doing is giving her ammunition. Remember, if your feelings counted, you wouldn't be talking divorce.

No fooling around. Stop any affairs, stay away from other women, and don't frequent strip bars or other sex industry locations. All of this will be used as evidence against you. If you are in love with someone else, and she loves you, then ask her to wait. She won't want to jeopardize your status in the divorce, because she is thinking of you first and not herself. No? Ah, I thought so. She is not concerned about your well-being. You're about to trade one owner for another. If she says yes she will wait, then you have a winner.

Get an attorney. Most men wait until it's an emergency. Get advice now on things to watch out for. Lay out a schedule of motions, papers and legal moves. You don't have to activate the schedule, just have an idea what it would be. Also, learn what you should not do—for example, moving out of the house may be taken as your agreement that it is hers.

Set a date. Know when you would make your move, whether it is approximate or definite. This will give you a light at the end of the tunnel.

Decide your custody stance. Be a good father, build your reputation; examine hers.

Stash some cash. You must have operating funds when you lower the boom (or if she surprises you). Have some money you can get without permission of her attorney, and get all of it the day everything goes down. You have a right to survive.

Get your own CPA. Have an accountant who can help you stash cash, prepare financially for the divorce, and value your assets. You do not have confidentiality with an accountant like you would with a lawyer, so don't let her know about your accountant.

Evaluate your leverage. Plan to squeeze her with threats, and know that you can back those threats up. Women almost always assume they have rights to more than men think they do. Know the answers, and have them at your fingertips.

Move with power. Hey Mr. Nice Guy, you may need to devastate her with the power of your plan all at once, before she has an attorney, and before she knows what kinds of things to ask for. She'll be reacting; you'll be acting. Have the news delivered while she is at work, so she'll be under pressure to act cool.

Hire a detective. See if you can catch her in anything that will be useful in negotiations.

Know your new address. If you will be moving out, pick the place and know what stuff you will take.

If she will be moving out, set a deadline and have your attorney draw up an agreement saying when she will be out, when she will give you the keys, and what she will be taking with her.

Take your vacation time. Take off work so you can execute your plan, guard your stuff, and make the calls you need to.

Get a counselor. Start counseling well before you execute your divorce plan, before the emotional pain gets too bad. You'll have help when the divorce comes.

Join a club. Get your new social life going now, so you'll have acquaintances when you leave her.

Keep your job. You don't need another big change. Make your new career plan for after the divorce, about one year.

Get rid of evidence. Delete emails, toss papers, throw out gifts, and trash that old computer.

Get a P.O. Box. You will need a place to receive attorney and CPA bills, and correspondence relating to your plan. You need this in advance, so she won't discover your plan.

Get in shape. Get yourself together now, including appearance, health, clothes, grooming and attitude. Get ready for your new life, and you'll feel like going for a new life.

Tell a friend. You'll need an ally with a level head. You're going to consider some crazy moves, and your friend can weigh things a little more objectively.

Project your income. What is she likely to siphon off? What will you have left? Make some educated guesses. If she is going to be a barracuda, hold off on starting a side business until after the divorce. If you start it now, she may lay claim to half the income from it—without taking on half the risk!

Plan on an extra job or side business. You'll want to be busy, and you may need extra money. Be sure you know whether she's likely to want half of your extra income. Postpone your extra income plan until after the divorce if you have to, but know what the plan is. Otherwise, start the extra income in advance so you can save up for divorce expenses.

Have a garage sale. Get cash for stuff she might get, and stow some of that cash away. You don't have to tell her your reason for the sale. It's just time to clean out a little (before she cleans you out).

Get a storage unit. Put your new furnishings in it. Store all new purchases for your new life. Stow away some items she won't notice missing.

Get a real estate agent. If you will have to sell the house, you can have it on the market right after the divorce. You'll also have a rough idea of the market price for it, based on the agent's input.

Plan your second vacation time. A few months into the divorce, have a getaway planned, either between jobs or on sick leave. If you used all your vacation time on executing your divorce plan, set up a long weekend at least. Go somewhere sexy. Clear your head and get ready for the new you.

Set up an office. This will be command central for your divorce. You'll need a computer, fax machine, paper and envelopes, a sleeping cot, a planning calendar and privacy. Set this up far in advance of executing your divorce plan. You'll have a place to work and sleep in case things get rough.

Sell your house and move now. Pick a state with better divorce laws, and plan a move for both of you. You can announce the divorce when you get there.

Take care of her. Have a plan in place for her. Plan her income, assets, and housing situation, and you may eliminate much of her resistance.

Devastate her. This is the opposite of "take care of her." Get nasty fast, to eliminate or minimize her retaliation. Ask for more than you want. Give her a vision of having nothing. That may cut her animosity back a notch.

Cash in bonds and investments. Cash is easier to divide. Take some off the top for operating capital.

Open your own checking account. You need the ability to pay your own bills privately.

Take a class. Learning brightens you. Learn about that subject she always mocked. Enroll before you announce the divorce, and you'll have a forward-looking mindset. This will be a good place to make new friends.

Prepare to have your best friend turn on you. If you think she cuts you down now, just wait until divorce is on the table. Hell hath no fury like a woman about to lose control of a man she thought she'd have under her thumb the rest of her life.

Be prepared to hear some nasty stuff about you. Don't let it surprise you out of your plan. Be prepared to go from nice guy to ass if she goes from best friend to barracuda.

Hire some help. You are suddenly going to be mailing all the bills, handling all the grocery shopping, cleaning the house, going to work, setting the doctor appointments—everything. Get a personal assistant for the transition. Advertise on Craigslist for someone to get you organized and help you make the transition. A day a week could do it until you get the hang of it.

These steps will help you make your divorce a positive part of your midlife crisis. Don't forget the MID in midlife crisis. You're only in the middle. You have a lot ahead of you. One day, your divorce will be a memory. How you handled it will mean a lot to you. Be a man. Go for greatness. Have the best divorce possible—that means making sure things go your way.

If you believe you have a purpose in life, a destiny, then this divorce is part of what it will take to get you to your ultimate destination.

This is a battle, and you are going to win it. Get tough. Get going. Get happy.

My friendly reminder:

I'm working on a great divorce—it will last longer than my marriage!

Chapter Eight

Extra Caution.

When you're being watched, know your spy stuff!

Are you being followed? Is someone watching all the keystrokes you make on your computer? Are the phone calls on your cell phone bill itemized so that someone can read them? Did someone find your password, and are they reading your private emails?

You are not paranoid. You are a middle-aged male, and many people consider you an appropriate subject for spying. There is a long tradition of not trusting middle-aged men. So don't trust people who don't trust you.

Now I'm not necessarily talking about covering your tracks for an affair. There are lots of things you may not be allowed to do, from bowling to drinking. If you cover your activities, you'll have a lot more peace in your life. And don't think having an affair is the only thing they'll come at you with at divorce proceedings. Hey, wasn't that you going into a bar? Weren't you seen coming out of an adult book store? Did you or did you not blow your family's hard-earned money playing pool last Saturday? It's all evidence against you. And if there's a woman involved, forget it. You're cooked.

You need some countermeasures. Hey, you've always wanted to be a spy anyway, so become Agent 001, looking out for number one.

Here are scenarios that may endanger you, and suggested ways to minimize your vulnerability.

You are Being Followed.

There is that same car. A guy across the street from your house pulls out when you do. You just have a feeling on the back of your neck that someone is watching you as you walk down the street. You've been taught not to trust your feelings. If women feel they're being followed, they are urged to have someone accompany them to the parking garage. If men feel they're being followed, they are urged to get psychiatric help.

Women hire private investigators all the time. But not your mate, right? Hmm. Then why are you feeling so uneasy?

Just in case, here is how to keep from getting busted.

1. Stop fooling around. If you are acquiring extra women, stop. Don't go anyplace questionable, like strip clubs. Put off the massage, and be a good boy. Private investigators are expensive. After a short period of no results, your mate will call him off.

2. Hire a private investigator. To follow you, not her. Get an extra pair of eyes on the scenery as you go out. Don't do anything risky, but break out of your usual routines. Stop for a beer, have dinner, go to a different part of town. Your investigator will know if her investigator is watching.

3. Look good being bad. Once you've convinced yourself the coast is clear, go have a good time. But do it differently. No

public places. Don't park your car somewhere you can't justify. Take a bus, take two busses. Don't use your cell phone or electronic personal assistant to make any arrangements. Change your meeting place. Pay cash for everything.
4. Go home. If you find out you were being followed, you have some serious changes to make. Divorce could be pending. Read the chapter on divorce and prepare for the worst. DO NOT engage in any extracurricular activities. It's time for the soldier in you to man up and get disciplined. Don't give anybody any evidence that will cost you. You can get back to your midlife crisis when you've got some power on your side. The divorce chapter will give it to you.

Your Computer is Being Checked.

When the internet started, it was wild and untamed. Now your computer remembers everything you do, stores deleted emails, and identifies you to people online even when you don't know it is doing so.

In addition, there is software a certain someone can easily install on your computer that records every single keystroke you make.

And don't even think about renting a computer at an internet cafe. You pay with a credit card that can be traced, and the computer has a record of what you've done.

Here's how to keep your computer from turning you in:
1. Go low tech. Talk to your secret person in person. Do it in a casual meeting place, where no one could have guessed you were going, so there won't be any way they could have set up a recording device. A low whisper is the best defense.

2. Make your computer anonymous. Websites identify you through your internet service provider. This includes the free email websites. They know who you are, and if pressed by a judge, may give you up. So let's hide you. First, get Firefox from the Mozilla website. Second, get Tor. Google it, and you'll find it easily. It is software that takes you to websites through proxy servers, hiding your internet provider information from the websites. Go through Tor to sign up for your new email account, and they won't have your internet provider to incriminate you.

3. Install anti-spyware and adware software. Whew! That's a mouthful. Here's the simple version. Websites follow you and report what you are doing. They know what sites you visit, how long you stay there, and how often you return. There is software to stop this. You have to have it. Google "anti spyware", and make your best choice. Have your computer checked by a technician to see if anyone has installed software to track your typing, and have it removed. Don't mention it to anyone. Now check it a week later. Is it back? Start using it. Find out what your little spy types when you're not around.

4. Sign up for a second email account. After you have installed Tor, use hotmail, yahoo, or one of the dozens of free email services. Never access it outside of the Tor program, and there will be no record of who you really are. Again, these services track your internet provider, and know who you are. But if you use Tor, there's no trail back to you. And of course, you use a different name. If the free email service wants an existing email address when you sign up, find a service that

doesn't ask for this, such as mail.com. Also don't use your real name in the bodies of your emails when you are writing to whoever it is you email. If someone claims it was you later, oh yeah? Says who?

5. Don't make secret arrangements on your regular cell phone or personal digital assistant—Blackberries, iPhones, etc. They can be easily traced and accessed. They are an electronic record of everything you do. .

Your Phone Records are Being Checked

Cell phone companies keep a record of every call you make. Even an amateur detective can easily find out who you have been talking to, how often, and how long. Buy a prepaid cell phone. Services like www.telestial.com sell them. Replace your phone periodically.

Also, you can get a voice mailbox through companies like onebox.com. They'll answer your phone calls for you, and you can decide which ones to call back. From your prepaid phone of course.

Your Credit Cards are Being Tracked.

Don't use credit cards for anything. Don't use credit cards for ANYTHING. DON'T use credit cards for anything. Have you read the news? There are so many prominent men who are busted because they use a credit card, it's a wonder guys don't get a clue. Don't use credit cards for anything.

GPS is Watching.

That stands for "global positioning system." It is the same technology that cars have to operate those dashboard maps. Many cell phones have them. Some handheld devices do. Many computers do. Blackberries, IPhones, all of your handheld devices that can find directions do it with GPS.

1. Have your devices checked for GPS devices and remove them. Why does anyone need to know where your cell phone is? But watch out, they can still find your phone by tracking the cell signal. Turn it off when you go to an incriminating part of town.

2. Leave the car where it belongs, if you can't dismantle the mapping system. Take alternate transportation. If you use a cab, use two cabs. If anyone asks the first driver where you went, they'll be at a dead end because you caught another cab from there. Bus drivers won't remember where you got off. Don't use a credit card to rent a second car. You'll leave a paper trail.

Smile for the Camera.

Cameras are everywhere. Hotels, ATMs, cell phones, parking structures, police cars (they film you if they stop you), even the car ahead of you has a camera in the rear for backing up. If you think someone could be overly interested in whether you are photogenic, you are in serious jeopardy. Here's what you do:

1. Disguise yourself. No, it is not silly. Wear a hat that covers your face. Wear clothes you would never wear. Walk differently. Don't look up. And here's a tip most people don't know about: change the disguise. Don't use any false identity that is consistent. People will have a hard time proving the guy in the white hat is the same guy in the black hat. Store a

second wardrobe somewhere—like a storage unit or rented locker-- and change after you leave the house.

2. Know your meeting place. Learn the camera placements at places you frequent. Look away, look down, take a different route around the cameras.

3. Change your habits. People have to know which cameras to check, because there are so many of them. Don't use the same ATMs, streets, hotels, parking lots or cafes. No one can check ALL the cameras in town!

4. Check the knick-knacks. Suddenly have a new teddy bear in the bedroom? A new clock, a picture frame? Cameras are being put into all kinds of knick-knacks these days, and if your house is suddenly acquiring lots of do-dads, you should check them for lenses.

An Irresistible Stranger Has to Have You.

She's a knockout. She wants your body now. Sounds like a set up. More than one suspicious mate has talked a friend into testing her man. More than one guy has been busted by cops who sent a beautiful girl to see if he'll make an offer. Use your other head. Here's what you do:

1. Have some fun. You're not falling for this. Play it for all it's worth. Talk up your mate. Tell her you are a happily controlled man. Say you have to go. Tell your stranger you hope she finds the happiness you've found. Won't you sound good when the report gets back to your mate?

2. Don't talk money. This could also be a vice squad set up. If you start saying, "How much?" you could get in trouble fast. Never talk money with an attractive stranger, in public or private.
3. Start a No-lip, No-Zip Affair. When a drop-dead female comes on to you, talk, be friendly, don't be seductive. If this is a legit situation, you'll know in a few days. No sex today. Just talk. Don't exchange numbers. Don't make a date to meet again. Just say you come here once in awhile, maybe you'll see her again. She'll be there if she really wants you. And to cover your butt, tell your mate later that this stranger just started talking to you. If your mate set it up, you'll look like Mr. Honest. If she didn't, at least you may make her a little jealous. That might rekindle something.

Your Money Trail is Being Followed.

Even though you use cash (no credit cards!), you can leave a paper trail. Don't leave any evidence of your presence. Here's how to erase your presence when you pay for things:

1. Don't sign receipts. Don't give anyone your name to put on a receipt they are giving you. Just forget the receipt, you don't need any proof you were there.
2. Don't leave big tips. Cash draws attention. The waitress will remember you. The bartender will too. Be discreet, don't make a show of not using a credit card. Put your money down and walk away.

3. Avoid huge ATM withdrawals. Few people know that the bank has a profile on each depositor, a risk rating. They will notify someone if you make unusual moves. And you thought it was your business and no one else's! The bank watches for unusual withdrawals, frequent withdrawals and any behavior that breaks a pattern. They could report you to Homeland Security, or just call home and talk to your wife. Put your fun money in a separate account at another bank, and establish withdrawal patterns there.

The Gifts You Give Give You Away.

Lots of guys get busted buying gifts for a special someone. There is nothing more embarrassing than having your gifts exposed! Here are some guidelines:

1. Don't brag to the clerk that you are buying this for your girlfriend. Your ego is going to bring you down. Be invisible. Be unmemorable. If the gift is expensive, pass it off as no big deal.
2. Don't buy duplicate gifts. Tons of dummies buy their wives and girlfriends the same gift! What a dead giveaway! If those gifts ever end up in the same room, you're sunk. Besides, the women will be insulted. They hate having the same thing as anyone else in the room.
3. Don't send flowers. That requires credit cards, names, a whole bunch of stuff you want to stay away from. Bring the flowers yourself.

4. Don't shop at the same place twice. Some nosy clerk will remark that "the lucky girl" is getting lots of presents. You just got noticed. You don't want to be noticed. Plus, it will seem odd that you paid cash again. Find a new store.
5. Don't shop where you buy your wife's gifts. You big dummy. You could accidentally end up in there with your wife some day, and you'll be trying to explain why you bought chocolates, no wait, was it diamonds? Oh, the clerk just reminded you, it was rubies and lace panties. Ouch! How are you going to explain when the clerk spills the beans?

You have Guilty Friends.

Friends are the biggest source of trouble. They will unwittingly bring you down. Or you may have a falling out and they turn on you. Here's how to protect yourself from friends:

1. Don't be a big shot. You just had to brag, didn't you? You were so insecure, you had to tell your buddy about your exploits, just to get that pat on the back. Now you are at someone else's mercy. The minute you say, "I trust," look out. "I trust" is the last phrase of the soon-to-be defeated. The more people know your business, the more likely you are to get in trouble.
2. Don't use friends as alibis. This old chestnut will do you in. Asking a friend to say you were with him makes him part of your subterfuge. That's not cool. If he's a friend, treat him with respect and don't put him in a position to lie for you. Reluctant liars give out eventually, and when they clear their consciences, you'll be clearing out your clothes.

Your Travel is Tripping You Up. Most travel requires ID, credit cards, hard-and-fast records. You can't easily get around it without alerting Homeland Security. Airlines won't let you travel anonymously, and most hotels won't accept you without ID.

The best thing to do is have a legitimate reason to go where you're going, a reason you can defend and explain easily. If you are dying to lie on the beach at Tahiti with your sweetie, get your divorce. Get free and do what you want. Never travel anywhere you don't want anyone to know you are going.

Sure, if you keep it fairly local, you can drive anonymously, kind of, if you pay cash for gas along the way. And if whoever you are meeting is willing to put a room in their name, that would hide you. Just don't make any ATM withdrawals nearby, or you'll leave a record of your presence. Don't rent a car for this, there will be a record of your mileage.

Still, there will be lots of cameras, records of turnpike tolls, a waitress at a coffee shop who may remember you, and possibly a global positioning system on your car (and definitely on the rental car).

The best way to travel, even by car, it to have a legitimate reason for the trip, then "piggy back" your extra activities onto that trip.

Working Late at the Office is Not Working. You have no expectation of privacy at the office. Your emails, phone calls and movements are all company business. There are too many prying eyes and too many gossips. Please don't be one of the fools who uses office equipment to make arrangements. Even a secretary saying, "He's been acting strange" can be used against you. Separate your work life from your secret life.

Why You Don't Need a Paper Shredder. You don't need one because you are never going to bring home an incriminating piece of paper. Why grab a receipt for something you want to hide? Don't stick it in your pocket thinking you'll shred it later. You don't need it. Don't try to write off these kinds of receipts on your tax return. Just let it go. If you are shredding paper, you are guilty of carrying incriminating paper. Don't carry it. Ever.

Now, if you feel you have to do ALL of these things, hold on a minute. That's way too serious. Stop all activity and get some professionals on your side. Go to the divorce plan and spring into action, even if you don't go all the way to divorce. She may. Someone who is watching you too much is either nuts or dangerously possessive or planning a divorce. Get some evidence, and don't give her any.

My friendly reminder:

I live it up so I'll have something to live down!

Chapter Nine

Extra Inspiration.

In the end, it's how you like who you were that matters!

While you're in the middle, imagine the end. Imagining your death bed can be one of the most rewarding experiences you can have. Knowing how you want to die tells you how to live.

If you envision being surrounded by your family who admires your lifelong steadfastness, your dedication to them while sacrificing your own life, then skip the midlife crisis, you're doing fine.

If you want to look back on a lifetime of serving others, even though you never went on that African safari, or built that commercial real estate empire, or sailed the ocean, then relax and serve, comforting yourself with the notion that other's dreams are more important than your own.

But wait. If helping others achieve their dreams is nobler, then those others should be helping you achieve your dreams. Yeah right. Try selling them on that one. Suddenly they won't think helping others is so noble.

"Honey, I know I helped you achieve your dream of having a home and a family. Now I'd like to work on my dream of going on an arctic expedition."

"What? You selfish bastard. You owe it to me and your family to stay here."

"But what about my dream?"

"Your dreams are foolish. Mine are sensible."

Got it. Whatever you want is wrong. So lie there on your deathbed looking back on a lifetime of regrets if you think that will be rewarding; the rest of us are going to grow some balls and get busy on our dreams.

Look, I know this book is provocative, but you're dying here. Do something that's lively. Get vigorous.

Glance ahead. There you are, an old man with days left to live. You look back and say, "What a life!"

What was it you did? Who was it you met?

Now come back to the present. You're relatively young, aren't you? Whew! There's still time! Get going. Have a great midlife crisis, and make it the springboard to a great rest of your life.

"Now, wait," they will say. "Patience is a virtue." The next time someone says that to you, say, "He who hesitates is lost."

And lost it is, my friend. Once you're at the end, you're at the end. It's over, and the chance to live is lost.

You've been patient up to now. Look what it got you. You're sitting there watching your life speed by, while people tell you to be patient. Next thing you know, you'll be a patient invalid watching the wheelchairs speed by, and you'll be sitting still, wondering what the hell happened.

Oh yeah, and, "Don't be angry. It's not good for you. It will raise your blood pressure. Besides, it's childish. You're just throwing a temper tantrum."

Here they are trying to take you life away and they don't want you to be angry. They're afraid you might get mad enough to change. They would much rather you take a pill, calm down and go on making *their* lives better.

Who's trying to make *your* life better? Oh yeah, the Great Sacrificer doesn't get a better life. Now don't get angry.

Baloney. Get mad. Get pissed. Get going.

This deathbed stuff can seem morbid, but really, I'm trying to shock you into action. The day WILL come!

So here's another one of my dares. Do a Google search on your dream. Want to move to Paris? Type in "Relocating to Paris." Guess what? People less timid than you have been thinking about it, writing about it, doing it. I typed in this phrase and got 258,000 results. So why is it so strange for you to think about it? What's the big deal? There are whole industries built around relocating to Paris. But not for the Great Sacrificer. You've got to stay put while everyone else goes where they want.

Let's try another one, maybe something really bad, secret, and off-the-wall. Hey, about "threesomes?" Ah, oh. Now that is really weird. Unthinkable. How dare you? Let's see, I got twelve million results. Twelve million. So this little secret fantasy is not a secret at all to millions of people. They're not sneaking around with fantasies locked away in their heads. No, that kind of torture is reserved for the Great Sacrificer. Sheesh. Who convinced you that everybody but you gets a life?

Look, I'm not saying you have to have a threesome, or move to Paris. Those are just examples. You might want something else, and that's fine, as long as it's what you really want. What I'm saying is that your wildest fantasies are just not that wild. Someone somewhere is already doing them! So dream big, and get out there. Wake up. You're young compared to that old guy who will be on the deathbed looking back. Give him something to smile about.

I will tell you the truth. I wrote this book in the middle of the wildest time of my life. It could have been a lot wilder, but I took time out to write once in awhile. I didn't go through all this just to sacrifice my time so you could fantasize about living a great life. I expect you to really do it. I wrote this to help some guys like me live a full life. Like me.

Keep this deathbed view in your head. It's not morbid, it's essential. On those days you feel like asking for what you want is silly, remember this vision.

Now, I am going to make it easier for you. I want you to fill out a Midlife Master Plan. It is a detailed set of actions you promise to take on your on behalf.

So get out your pen and mark the next chapter up. Fill it in, cross it out, rewrite it. Write in the margins. Get something on paper about how you are going to live before it's too late!

My friendly reminder:

We learn from our mistakes, so I make as many as possible!

Your Midlife Master Plan

Let's Separate the Men from the Boys.

Write it down and put it into action!

This is the part of the book I want you to write. This is your life story, the life ahead of you.

This is your Midlife Master Plan. It's about your goals and guidelines, and for once nobody's going to tell you how to plan your life. These sections are your place to begin real steps to a fuller life.

Fill them out, and at the end you'll have a complete Midlife Master Plan for changing your life!

Wait a second. I know you. You're don't take yourself seriously enough. Why would a plan work now, when all your plans have led you to a midlife crisis?

Now stick with me on this. Fill out the Midlife Master Plan sections, start doing what you promise yourself you'll do, and we're really, *really* going to win together!

This is not dreaming, this is doing. You are going to come out on top, and soon!

Your Extra Women Plan

Time to decide your course of action or inaction regarding women.

Choose which of the following expresses where you are regarding extra women:

1. I'm going to make some good female friends.
2. Hell, I'm at least going to go one step further and see if I want to back out.
3. You kidding? I'm in. I'm going to look for some low-risk situations.

Now do some logistics:

I will begin doing this on this date _____

The place I will do this is _____

The amount of money I can use on this is $_____

They type of person I will do this with is _____

My acceptable risk is (use the rating list from the "Extra Women" chapter) _____

I will bail out if this happens
_____
_____
_____
_____
_____

I promise not to feel guilty for finding out what I really want.

Your Extra Money Plan.

Circle your choices.

1. I Will Keep My Job. (Quit stressing over it, it's temporary.)
2. I will make a budget that includes fun and investments. Budget to be finished by (date) _____
3. This is the amount of extra money I need for my midlife crisis, including money for fun and investing $_____
4. I will earn that extra money through:
    a. Business income Amount $_____
    b. Investment growth Amount $_____
    c. Both—the amounts I expect from each are:
        i. business $_____
        ii. investments $_____
5. I will replace my job with
    a. A better job;
    b. A new business.
6. I plan to escape from debt by adjusting the 50/50 fun/investing plan to a 33/33/33 fun/investing/debt-reduction plan. This will apply $_____ to debt, $_____ to fun, and $_____ to investing.
7. I plan to get away from my current situation, whether job, relationship, or location, by (date) _____.
8. I will open a secret account so I can disappear by (date) _____
9. That account will be located in _____

Your Extra Creativity Plan

This is the one you are most likely to let slip. Most people look upon creativity as an extra in life.

Look, I'm not fooling around here. I don't want you to just think about changing things, I want you to really do it. Now. Today. Change one thing. Just one. I dare you.

So let's get real about this. I want you to complete the following sentences.

1. Today I will do something I've never done before, which is

_____
_____
_____
_____
_____

_____

2. I am going to look at mistakes I've made, and see them as something I did right by seeing myself as:

_____
_____
_____
_____

3. One way I've never thought of to make money is

_____

4. Women would treat me differently if I just believed that I

_____

5. A fun thing I haven't done in too long is

_____

6. Something I've never tried that sounds fun is
_____

7. If I really focused and believed in myself, I could
_____

8. The lifestyle that really fits me is
_____

9. If I spent ninety days doing _____, it would change my life.

10. If my life up to now were a novel, here is how the second half would surprise readers:

_____
_____
_____
_____
_____

Okay, you get the idea. Use those ten sentences as thought-starters. Write ten more of your own. You don't have to have all the answers, just ask some fantastic questions.

Write "What if ..." on a piece of paper ten times, and complete it ten different ways.

List the three things you hate about your life and imagine ways to get rid of them. Be wild with your strategies. It's only words. You can crumple up the paper later.

Your Toys and Adventure Plan

Make some decisions for *you:*

Here are the top three toys I want to either buy or rent:
1.
2.
3.

This will cost $_____.

I plan to have that money together by (date) _____.
I will have my first toy by (date) _____
Second toy by _____
Third toy by _____

The top three places I want to go are:
1.
2.
3.
This will cost $_____.
I will have this money by (date) _____.
I will book my first trip by (date) _____.

Some in-town things I have been wanting to do are:
1.
2.
3.

I will do #1 on this date: _____

I will do #2 on this date _____

I will do #3 on this date _____

I will consider a Mate Date, by asking my wife to go to _____ on _____ (date).

A trip I'd like to plan with the guys is:

I will call _____ (friend) about this trip on _____(date).

A sport I have always wanted to try or have always enjoyed is:

I will start playing this sport on (date) _____.

The equipment and preparations I need for this are:

I have always wanted to take a course in
_____
_____
_____
_____

I will sign up for my first course by (date) _____.

Some places I could find such a course are:

Learning Annex

Local colleges

Meetup.com groups who could recommend

Through an expert I could call

Other _____

_____

_____

_____

_____

Your Midlife Health Plan

Your commitment: I plan to get tough.

Second commitment: I promise I will also have fun while I am improving my health.

I will start my exercise program on this date: _____.

The time of day I will do it is _____.

The number of times per week I will do it is _____.

I will go shopping for testosterone-boosting foods on _____ (date).

I will insist that these foods be part of home meals.

I am beginning my mental workout now. The areas I most want to improve are (circle those that apply):

Memory

Problem-solving

Perceiving details

Vocabulary and writing

Listening

Mental reaction time

Math ability

My first mental exercise is to come up with the following resources for boosting my mental workout.

Resources I could use:

(Examples: crossword puzzle book, word power book, games, etc)

_____
_____
_____
_____
_____
_____

Emotions. I am taking charge of my emotions. They do not drive me, I drive them.

I will practice considering my reactions to others, including my mate.

I will see a professional on (date) _____ .

My stress-reduction ideas are:

_____
_____
_____
_____
_____

I have decided to take Sam-e and vitamin B. I will begin this regimen on (date): _____.

The top three people who have wronged me are:

_____

_____

_____

Some ways I could get even with them without hurting myself are:

_____
_____
_____
_____
_____
_____
_____
_____

I will choose one of the above ideas and implement it on (date) _____.

The easiest ways to get more sex into my life are:

_____
_____
_____
_____
_____

I will start doing one or more of these on (date) _____.

I promise to protect my health and the health of my sexual partner(s).

I need help in the hard-on department. I will see a urologist by (date) _____.

I promise to keep my health insurance premiums paid on time.

Your Marriage or Significant Relationship Plan

My marriage is lopsided—it's based on my commitments without enough talk of her commitments.

I will sit down and talk to my mate about her commitments in this relationship, including her commitment to:

My dreams

Debt reduction

Building my self-esteem

Honoring my alone time

Honoring my financial freedom (personal cash)

Honoring my masculinity (quit whining when I look at women)

Planning spending together—I am not your employee

Planning for fun

Honoring my desire for guy time

Eliminating financial meanness from divorce discussions

Clearing up custody issues in the event we don't make it

Your Divorce Plan

I need to plan my divorce so I can keep from being devastated. Here's what I need to do. Circle all that apply.

Clean up my act so there's less evidence against me

See an attorney to discuss my vulnerability

Set a date for the divorce _____

Open an account for my cash at (name of bank) _____

See a CPA for tips on stashing cash and protecting assets

Hire a detective

Choose the place I will live

Get a counselor to prepare myself

Join a club to expand my social life

Get rid of things I don't want her to find, whether paper or electronic

Ask for my vacation time so I can execute the plan

Get a P.O. Box

Start getting in shape for single life

Discuss this with a friend

Plan a business for after the divorce

Have a garage sale

Get a storage unit

Choose a real estate agent

Set up an office as command central

Cash in investments

Take a class on something she disapproves of

Make my power move on (date) _____

Take my second vacation to get away from the divorce stress on (date) _____

I want you to make two lists.

Your divorce strengths. List all the things you have on your side in the divorce. What areas are you strong in, and what areas can you strengthen? Are you a good planner, a ruthless negotiator? Or maybe your income earning potential is a strength. Get your arsenal inventoried. What are the things that are going to help you win in this divorce? Do you know a great attorney? Do you have friends who will help you? Think. Come up with ten strengths.

My Divorce Arsenal

_____   _____
_____   _____
_____   _____
_____   _____
_____   _____

Your personal strengths. Maybe you make friends easily. Or maybe you tell good jokes. What are the good things she is overlooking? What is it someone else will find attractive? List all the positive qualities that will help you be a great person after the divorce.

Think of ten things your wife has overlooked or underplayed.

My Personal Positives

_____   _____
_____   _____
_____   _____
_____   _____
_____   _____

Your Spy Stuff Plan

I will start trusting my instincts, and my instincts tell me
_____
_____

_____
_____
_____
_____

I am taking these measures to see if I am being followed:
_____
_____
_____
_____
_____

Here are some ways I can communicate without computers or personal assistants:
_____
_____
_____
_____
_____

A good place to sit and talk to someone privately is: _____

On my computer, I will either install Firefox and Tor, or I will have a technician do it for me. This will be done by (date) _____ .I will sign up for an anonymous email account with (service) _____ .

Here is a list of all devices I use that may have a global positioning system in them.

_____
_____
_____
_____

I will buy a prepaid cell phone at (website or store)
_____

I have counted all the cameras I notice in the places I go. Here's what I saw:
_____
_____
_____
_____
_____

One place I know I could go that has no cameras is:
_____

Some clothes I could stash as a disguise are:
_____
_____

A place I could stash those clothes is:
_____

If a beautiful woman comes on to me, my plan is to

_____
_____
_____
_____
_____

I am going strictly cash for everything I want to keep to myself.

I will buy extra gifts at (name of store) _____.

My best cover story for a travel trip is:

_____
_____
_____
_____
_____

_____

I will not use the office for any personal communications I want kept secret.

I will not keep any piece of paper I don't want anyone to read. (Memorizing phone numbers can become part of my mental workout!)

Your End-of-Life Vision

When I look back on my life, the thing that will make me smile is that I really did this:

_____
_____
_____
_____
_____

122

There, that's the beginning of your Midlife Master Plan. Email me to tell me how it's going. Come to www.ManUpMen.wordpress.com and share with others who are going through what you are going through. You can ask questions, express concerns, or just SHOUT OUT LOUD about how much fun you're having.

Welcome back to life!

Extra Resources to Make Midlife Better

You Need All the Help You Can Get.

Assemble your weapons for the battle ahead!

Go to www.ManUpMen.wordpress.com for updates and resources, as well as to talk to others like you. Also sign up on the site to be notified when these are published:

"Secret Money Places" Where to hide money, and how.

How to Finance Your Midlife Crisis Workbook. A thorough method that will help you get your finances in order and moving in a prosperous direction!

Mission Finder—An Interactive Workbook to Help You Find Your Purpose. You'll be able to identify the work or business that suits your mission.

Best Sports Bars of All Time. Great companion for your trips!

How to Disappear in Midlife

Printed in Great Britain
by Amazon.co.uk, Ltd.,
Marston Gate.